Stewart,

"Blinded by the Phone"

not any more.

Enjoy Balls!

Ed Jachim

Employee #12

Pg 129

Stewart

"Blinded by the phone"
not any more.

Enjoy Bells 🔔

Employee #12
Pg 124

Advance Praise for *Balls!* by Alexi Venneri

"*Balls!* will inspire you. It's a guide for revving up the passion in your workplace. You'll discover how to enhance your sales processes, motivate your employees, and pursue your company's full potential. Read this profound book and your spirit will bounce back."

—Dan Fine, president, Fine Business Solutions

"This book is addictive. I started skimming it and then drilled down into the examples, ideas, and new-think approaches. I found it engaging and motivational. *Balls!* is packed with real-world examples of how to leverage existing assets, whether they are human assets, technological assets, or financial assets. Read this book. It will make a difference for you and your company."

—Larry Chase, publisher of *Web Digest for Marketers* and author of *Essential Business Tactics for the Net*

"*Balls!* is a testament to the courage it takes to never take no for an answer. It's about having more than assertiveness, resiliency, and determination. Coaches and leaders from all disciplines will be inspired to see things in their team that their players don't even see in themselves."

—Dwane Casey, assistant head coach, Seattle Sonics

"An extremely successful blend of storytelling, advice, and wisdom. It's an inspiring book filled with useful anecdotes and marvelously detailed case studies, presented with humor and intelligence."

—Lou Tice, founder of The Pacific Institute and author of *Smart Talk*

"Being Brave, Authentic, Loud, Lovable, and Spunky simply makes sense. Put these qualities together and you get a winning combination for any game. This innovative book is like getting a pep talk from your favorite coach."

—Mark Spangler, president and CEO,
The Spangler Group

"Who wouldn't want to have *Balls!*? It's quick, it's fun, and it's inspirational. Consider *Balls!* a must-read for entrepreneurs and executives from all disciplines."

—Ted Loughead, president,
Loughead Automotive Group

"If you want to become a successful leader in business today, you must commit yourself totally to your company and to your company's customers. You must be an enthusiastic and credible cheerleader for your company at all times. You must be a positive and energizing role model, both inside and outside the company. Alexi Venneri is just this type of role model—bold, creative, and caring."

—Jeffrey J. Fox, author of
How to Become a Rainmaker, How to Become a
Great Boss, and How to Become CEO

6 Rules for Winning Today's Business Game

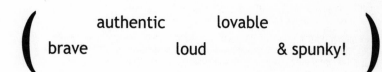

(authentic   lovable

brave   loud   & spunky!)

Alexi Venneri

WILEY

John Wiley & Sons, Inc.

Published by John Wiley & Sons, Inc., Hoboken, New Jersey.
Published simultaneously in Canada.

For general information on our other products and services please contact our Customer Care Department within the United States at (317) 572-3993 or fax (317) 572-4002.

Wiley also publishes its books in a variety of electronic formats. Some content that appears in print may not be available in electronic books. For more information about Wiley products, visit our web site at www.Wiley.com.

Library of Congress Cataloging-in-Publication Data:
Venneri, Alexi, 1971–
        Balls! : 6 rules for winning today's business game / Alexi Venneri.
             p. cm.
        Includes bibliographical references and index.
        ISBN 0-471-71272-8 (pbk.)
        1. Success in business—Handbooks, manuals, etc.   I. Title: 6 rules for winning today's business game.   II. Title.
        HF5386.V46 2005
        658.4'09—dc22
                                                                2004022895

Printed in the United States of America.
10 9 8 7 6 5 4 3 2 1

Balls! is dedicated to everyone who has ever truly believed they could win and then had the balls to actually do whatever it takes—whether that means painting your face with blue dots, braving a logo tattoo room, wearing four-foot fairy wings, sliding down a fire pole to your theme song, donning a crazy feather hat, buying a tuxedo shirt for a shipping-popcorn-filled mannequin, staying nine-to-a-house without power or heat, throwing hundred-dollar bills into a model-filled pool, or lowering yourself in a cage 30 feet down to a dance floor covered in boa-draped clients.

(Under the Cover)

Foreword

The Ascent of the Lovecat
by Tim Sanders

Over the past couple of years it's become obvious that many people running or managing business organizations have their priorities all mixed up.

It's really not surprising, when you consider what they've been reading in books or hearing from consultants. For quite a while, it seemed, anyone striving for success in business was encouraged to adopt the traits of bloodthirsty, violent predators. Business books and management gurus urged leaders to emulate the habits of sharks, barracudas, and piranhas.

I'm happy to report that most people now consider this type of misguided advice to be hopelessly out of date. Sharks, barracudas, and piranhas are on the way down. Nice, smart, loving people—people I call lovecats—are on the way up in the business world.

Again and again, I have found that the people in today's business world who are the most successful, the most appreciated, and the most satisfied are the lovecats. Simply defined, lovecats are people who share their knowledge, their networks, and their compassion with their business partners.

Guided by their intelligence and their good sense, lovecats share these three intangibles as widely as possible. Why do they share their love so freely? Because the old laws of supply and demand don't apply in most competitive zones of the New Economy. The old laws said that scarcity created value. Today, the opposite can be true. Abundance and ubiquity create value.

Sharing a great idea makes it a more valuable idea. *Including* more people in your network makes it a more valuable network. *Distributing* your compassion more widely makes it more likely that people will respond to you with compassion.

Think about the most successful companies of the New Economy and you'll see immediately what I mean. The best companies today don't measure success by market share or by victories over the competition. They measure success by the strength, quality, and value of their relationships with their customers. These companies apply love to the marketplace—and they profit from it.

In my book, *Love Is the Killer App*, I show clearly how love can be a point of differentiation in business. I show how love—in the business sense—can become an effective and sustainable competitive advantage.

Let's face it: Love is a winning strategy. It always was and it always will be. What I find especially worthwhile about Alexi's book is its cheerful willingness to embrace this essential concept, construct a robust business model around it, and offer specific examples of how love-based business strategies succeed in the real world.

Alexi has properly identified key traits of compassionate business organizations. They must be brave, authentic, loud, lovable, and spunky. They also must be willing to act decisively and consistently on their values and principles. In a very real sense, Alexi is helping all of us to define a new notion of corporate character—a character whose bedrock values reflect the core human values of our culture.

Alexi is most definitely a lovecat. She's a role model for a new generation of managers and executives who understand the value of their humanity in a rapidly changing business world. Ideally, her book will inspire more people to share their knowledge, their networks, and their compassion. Long live the lovecats!

Tim Sanders is the leadership coach at Yahoo! and author of the *New York Times* best-selling book *Love Is the Killer App: How to Win Business and Influence Friends*. His second book, *The Likeability Factor*, will be published in April 2005 by Crown Publishing.

"If you must play, decide on three things at the start:
the rules of the game, the stakes, and the quitting time."

~ Chinese Proverb

(Before the Book)

Twenty thousand dollars worth of rubber. Yes, $20,000. That's what it cost, in August of 2000, to buy 10,000 blue, rubber, blinking balls. I bought 10,000 and wasn't sure if I had enough. I wanted more. I'd been told that we were going to meet more than 17,000 car dealers in Las Vegas in just four days. And I wanted to give them all balls.

I was consulting for a company that didn't have a real logo, it didn't have a brochure, and it didn't have anything other than a functional web site that displayed reports. It certainly didn't have a trade show booth or a marketing plan. It *did* have a funny name, 12 employees, and a few hundred clients.

At the time I was also working for a major league baseball team so maybe, just maybe, I had balls on my mind. But I also knew that to not attend, to not exhibit, but to descend upon and take no prisoners at one of the largest trade shows in the country would take a helluva lot of balls.

I couldn't imagine doing anything else. The owner didn't blink when the CFO questioned him on my purchase. I hadn't asked him, and he didn't question me. Instead he simply stated, "Let's find out what we can do with that many balls." At that moment, I knew without question that I had to be employee 13.

Five years, nearly 300 employees, 7,000 clients, and more than 500,000 balls later, it has become obvious that a few simple rules can help you win the business game. You just need to be brave, authentic, loud, lovable, and spunky! Put those traits together and they spell *BALLS!*

So how do you grow your business and your bottom line and keep your investors happy and grow your business even more without going crazy in the process? How can you establish your brand in a fiercely competitive market—without spending a gazillion dollars on advertising? How do you build a ferociously competitive organization that honors human values? How do you manage a corporate culture that blends Spartan financial discipline with wild, off-the-wall creativity?

If these kinds of questions keep you up at night, first of all, you are probably working way too hard. My advice is to stop worrying about the details. Instead, start *paying attention* to them and make them work for you.

Ask any successful manager in major league baseball and he'll tell you that a winning season is built one game at a time. It's the same in business: Successful organizations focus their energies on achieving a series of short-term goals, over time. Great leaps come from taking a thousand small steps each day.

Throw away all those old, boring business strategy books. Take a break from the standard noise. Find out how some feisty businesses are not only surviving, but thriving in today's business world. Join our team and let's play ball.

In fact, let's not just play. Let's win!

(Snag the Ideas!)

All of the companies you are going to read about have come up with some really, really bad ideas. But by playing the business game over time, they've all discovered some really, really great ideas. And now you will, too.

Maybe you bought this book because you got to the airport two hours early and this time the security line took only two minutes. Maybe you haven't paid for the book yet and you're just reading it right now over a cappuccino at your bookstore. Maybe you're buying books with unusual titles to fill up a really cool bookcase in your office.

Well, here's the good news: You don't have to read every word in this book. If you're like me, you'll probably just want to hunt down a few good ideas that you can use to make your company better. Or use to make yourself look great.

That's fine with me. Take the good ideas you find

here and make them your own. Sometimes it takes only a couple of good ideas to make a lot of money.

We're going to make it as easy for you as possible. At the end of every chapter is a section called "Snag the Ideas!" Look for the ball—in fact, keep your eye on the ball—and snag the ideas that follow. And then maybe, just maybe, tell everyone you did—because that's ballsy!

Rule ❶ — B is for Brave

Brave. That is where it all starts. In business, you have to be brave to even seriously *think* about starting a new venture. You have to be brave to tell someone about it. You have to be brave to get someone to buy into it. You have to be brave to quit your nine-to-five job and strike out on your own. To win the game, you first must be brave enough to play it.

("To be **courageous** requires no exceptional qualities, no magic formula....It is an **opportunity** that sooner or later is presented to us all.")

~ John F. Kennedy

The Man in the Hawaiian Shirt

You would never confuse Lonnie Benson with Indiana Jones or any other action hero. But I consider him one of the bravest guys I've ever met.

Lonnie is the founder of Who's Calling. Yes, he's the

guy who lets me spend a lot of money on blue rubber balls. Guided by Lonnie's vision, Who's Calling has shot from $300,000 to $60 million in annual revenues in just a few short years.

To his credit, Lonnie doesn't act the part of a wealthy entrepreneur. If you run into Lonnie in downtown Seattle, he's likely to be wearing shorts, sandals, and a funky Hawaiian shirt. He smiles easily and appears relaxed. But there's a hint of rebellion in his eyes, something that says, "Don't tell me it can't be done."

Local Calling Hero

Lonnie Benson was born in 1956, delivered into life by a Navy obstetrician at an Army hospital in Seattle. His father, an electrical engineer, was serving with the Air Force in Korea. Lonnie didn't see him until he was six months old. By then, according to a journal kept by his mom, Lonnie was already fascinated with phones. "I guess it was the sound of human voices coming out of the receiver in the handset that really grabbed my attention," he recalls. "My mom says I was practically addicted to playing with the telephone."

Fast-forward to October 1987. "I was three months behind on my rent, unemployed, broke, and hungry. I was one small step away from living on the street. But I

BALLS!

had an idea. I knew that if I started my own small local phone company, I could take business away from the big local phone company."

Here was Lonnie's opportunity: telephone traffic between Seattle and nearby Tacoma was heavy. Many people living in Seattle consider Tacoma "local," but in fact these communities are in two different local calling areas.

The big local phone company, U.S. West (now Qwest Communications), charged callers up to 25 cents *per minute* for calls between the two local calling areas, meaning that if you lived in Seattle and wanted to chat with your sister in Tacoma, you had to either talk very fast or pay a hefty phone bill at the end of the month.

Lonnie needed cash to turn this opportunity into a business. By luck, and by living in a basement suite below a mutual friend, he happened to cross paths with a guy named Dan Horton. Dan was new to Seattle. Lonnie hardly knew him and he hardly knew Lonnie. But after a couple of nights of brainstorming and bar-hopping, Dan realized that Lonnie was onto something big.

Dan, to his eternal credit, handed Lonnie the cash he needed, just $350, to launch his first company, PhoneLink.

Now it was up to Lonnie to deliver. By now, he'd

learned just about everything he could about the existing telephone system—and he was ready to outsmart it!

By law, U.S. West was allowed to treat calls from one local calling area to another as toll calls. Lonnie found a location roughly between Seattle and Tacoma where he could set up an electronic bridge between the two local calling areas. His homegrown bridge essentially transformed what would have been expensive toll calls into inexpensive local calls. Then he created a very simple switching system to handle the calls, using an old IBM 286 PC that he programmed himself to emulate a telephone network. Unlike U.S. West, Lonnie charged callers just 25 cents *per call*. Whether you talked for a minute or an hour, you still paid 25 cents.

He of course needed a way to market his creation. "Some guy came to me and said for $300 he could mail my promotion to 10,000 people. I gave him $150 in telephone credit and a check for $150, which fortunately he didn't cash for a couple of days. The next Monday after the mailing went out, I started getting 10 to 15 phone calls a day. We charged $20 to sign up and our phone never stopped ringing. It just took off like a rocket and kept going straight up."

Lonnie kept expenses low by resisting the urge to spend money on fancy new equipment. He wrote a billing pro-

BALLS!

gram that ran on the IBM 286 during odd hours of the night when the little computer wasn't busy handling phone calls. Instead of buying an expensive printer to churn out bills and invoices, he daisy-chained six low-cost Panasonic KXP4450 printers to achieve the same results.

"Early on I made a critical decision," Lonnie recalls. "I simply refused to spend more money than I was taking in. It doesn't sound like a big idea, but it's been a basic element of our formula for doing business. With the exception of the cash we borrowed to get started, we avoided borrowing money. As a consequence of that decision, we had no debt."

The sudden popularity of PhoneLink also forced Lonnie to reevaluate his self-image. "I'd always thought of myself as some kind of techie. After PhoneLink caught on, I started hearing stories from people about how it had changed their lives. An elderly woman told me she had been paying $170 a month in toll charges because she wanted to stay in touch with her daughter, who lived a few towns away and was going through chemotherapy. PhoneLink lowered her phone bills to $5 a month, which made a huge difference in both their lives. They didn't care about the technology. They wanted to spend more time on the phone with each other and I was making that possible. That's when I stopped seeing myself as a lone-wolf techno-geek and started seeing myself as a businessman providing valuable services to people at reasonable prices."

Within a year, Lonnie's start-up was raking in profits exceeding $100,000 per month. "I went from the depths of poverty to making more money than I had ever dreamed possible within a very brief span of time. It was like one of those old movies where the poor guy suddenly strikes it rich."

Find the Gaps and Jump Right In

There's no question that PhoneLink's initial success relied on Lonnie's gut instinct and technical insight. But Lonnie wasn't the only guy in Seattle who figured out how to wire together a telephone bridge. Back in the 1980s, phone service across the Pacific Northwest was notoriously expensive. The high cost created a subculture of fly-by-night pirates offering hard-pressed consumers alternatives to the Baby Bells. Most of the pirates had a "take what you can and give nothing back" mentality, and vanished after making a quick buck.

Lonnie didn't just take the money and run. He was having too much fun! He perceived correctly that PhoneLink could be grown beyond its beginnings as an improvised platform for inexpensive phone service. His crucial insight was that PhoneLink, despite its questionable status on the margins of the telecom industry, was not a pirate. It was a business. Even so, PhoneLink was unusual for a start-up—it defied the odds and continued

BALLS!

to grow, without a significant line of credit or substantial backing from investors.

Two years after its launch, PhoneLink had 25,000 faithful customers happily paying 25 cents per call. And they were making lots of calls. Lonnie figured that his operations were costing U.S. West between $3 and $4 million in lost revenue every month.

"That's when I got the proverbial knock on the door," he recalls. "The utilities commission ruled that if I wanted to stay in business, I would have to become a registered telecommunications carrier. I guess they figured I would just go away. But instead of arguing with them, I went out and bought the equipment we needed to become a legally authorized long distance carrier."

You gotta love a guy who isn't afraid of the utilities commission and turns lemons into lemonade. In retrospect, it's clear that PhoneLink succeeded where other start-ups failed because of Lonnie's remarkable ability to identify small gaps in the market that had the potential to grow into large opportunities—and because he was brave to act swiftly enough to get an early jump on the competition.

I like to think of it in surfing terms. You can spend all day at the beach waiting for the perfect wave, or you can jump in and ride a not-so-perfect wave to hone your skills. Riding a series of small, imperfect waves won't land you on the cover of your favorite surfing magazine, but you'll be ready for the big wave when it finally comes.

The Amazing Vans

Following a hunch that the newly energized telecom industry would grow rapidly to encompass more than telephony, Lonnie changed the company's name from PhoneLink to Fox Communications. "The new name had a certain ring to it—no pun intended," says Lonnie.

True to Lonnie's wandering spirit, Fox Communications morphed, transformed, and reinvented itself to keep pace with the evolving telecom market. Then the advent of the cellular phone as a popular consumer item inspired Lonnie and his team at Fox to leap toward an entirely new wave.

The evolutionary path from PhoneLink to Fox Communications to Who's Calling was by no means a straight line. It wasn't even a paved road. There were unexpected side trails, blind alleys, 12 other companies, dead ends, shortcuts, and wormholes.

One of the wormholes appeared in the spring of 1996. Previously, cellular phones had been used mostly by businesspeople for business communications. By the

BALLS!

middle of 1996, it seemed as though everyone suddenly had a cell phone and was using it all the time.

When Fox Communications stepped into the cellular market, Lonnie quickly discovered that marketing cellular telephony wasn't much different from marketing landline telephony: Most of the dollars spent on marketing seemed to go nowhere. And that made him think. Lonnie was never one to accept the status quo. He was determined to find the most cost-effective way to market his cellular phone services. Direct mailing wasn't the right approach. TV, radio, and billboards seemed too expensive. There had to be a different way.

Lonnie thought it over. It's important to explain right now that Lonnie's thought processes are not linear. He has attention deficit disorder, which makes it difficult for him to perform some of the straightforward tasks that you or I might take for granted. He can't play chess, read 1,200-page Russian novels, or sit through three-hour business meetings.

But Lonnie Benson has learned to honor and respect the flashes of inspiration that illuminate his brain like bolts of lightning on a dark summer night. When one of those bolts arrives, Lonnie Benson pays attention to it. That's how he's different from most of us, and that's why we've all got something to learn from him. He also believes that anyone can catch a bolt of lightning—they're everywhere. You can often hear him saying, "You don't have to be Bill Gates brilliant to be a billionaire." And he really means it.

In this instance, Lonnie's idea involved assembling a fleet of wildly decorated vans to advertise his company instead of paying other people for space on their regular billboards. Some of the vans featured huge pictures of tropical fish. Others were adorned with pictures of giant keyboards. Big and bold was the only rule. Some of the designs were assembled from ultrareflective sheets of plastic that could be seen at night from miles away.

Simultaneously odd and irresistible, the vans appealed to Lonnie's maverick sensibilities. "I also liked the fact that you could build equity in the vans and that I controlled everything. What other kind of media lets you do *that*?"

A Last-Minute Detail That Changed the World

Wally Rex, who now runs client relations at Who's Calling, was hired specifically to unleash Lonnie's fleet of 60 vans on Seattle. He recalls how Lonnie added an extra, last-minute detail to the plan:

"Lonnie decided to put a different toll-free number on each van. We could do that because we're a phone company. I'd go out and park the vans all over town, or keep

BALLS!

driving them around until we found an area that would get some calls. If a van was generating calls, I'd leave it parked where it was. If the van wasn't generating calls, I'd run out and just keep driving it around until the calls started. Pretty soon, we knew exactly where to park the vans for maximum impact. And we were making deals with restaurants, 7-Elevens, and parking lots all over town."

Every night, Wally would log onto the company's billing system and carefully analyze the pattern of calls from the toll-free numbers on the vans. Over time, the ad hoc plan turned into an extremely effective marketing technique for Fox Communications. But another bolt of lightning was about to strike.

"At the time I really didn't care who was making the calls," admits Wally. "I was happy to know which vans were delivering returns on our investment and which weren't. To me, the vans were just big movable billboards."

One night, as Wally reviewed a day's worth of calling records, Lonnie walked past his desk. Then he stopped and turned around. In a flash, Lonnie realized that his van-based ad campaign had the potential to become much more than just a one-time business tactic. It could be the basis for a whole new enterprise, and maybe even a whole new industry. He suddenly had the answer to the age-old question, "I know half of my advertising is wasted, but the trouble is, which half?"

"Lonnie saw immediately that if we could track the response to the ads on our vans, we could do the same thing for other companies," says Wally. "And he saw that the technique wasn't limited to vans. It could be applied to marketing everywhere, for any business. That's when Who's Calling was born."

Five years later, Who's Calling has grown from less than $1 million to more than $60 million in annual revenue. We've pioneered a new industry. Today we not only track advertising and record calls—we partner with our clients, helping them leverage calls into sales transactions for more revenue at less expense. Our success was made possible by Lonnie's willingness to act bravely.

Lonnie overcame his own limitations and inhibitions. He persuaded a legion of doubters. He stood up to a large, established telecom. He was named one of Ernst & Young's Entrepreneurs of the Year. The Better Business Bureau keeps giving him awards. His company has been listed as one of the top five fastest-growing privately held businesses three years running and is now listed in the local Fastest Growing Hall of Fame. He battled the state of Washington. And he won.

Lonnie has balls.

BALLS!

Friendlier Skies

In business, being brave often means flying in the face of prevailing wisdom. Genuine bravery almost always involves taking risks. Entrepreneurs risk their capital, their time, and their reputations. Everything they own—tangible and intangible—usually goes on the table at one point during the process of launching a new business.

New York–based Marquis Jet Partners was brought to life by brave people who were willing to take risks—and accept the consequences of their gamble. Here's their story.

Back in 2000, two aggressive young entrepreneurs, Kenny Dichter and Jesse Itzler, decided to make the skies friendlier for hip-hoppers, sports stars, and Wall Street types. Contrary to popular belief, not all entertainers, athletes, and entrepreneurs are wealthy enough to own a personal jet. In fact, most aren't even wealthy enough to own shares or fractions of private jet planes.

Consider this: The up-front fee for a one-quarter share in a Gulfstream V is $10.1 million. Even the smallest fraction available, a one-sixteenth share in a Cessna Citation Excel, costs $620,000 and only entitles you to fly 50 hours per year!

So if you were a mere celebrity and not a megastar—or if you were a megastar without a mega-ego—there was no practical way to avoid the hassles of commercial jet travel without spending millions.

Kenny and Jesse have numerous friends in the sports and music industries. In 2001, they saw a clear opportunity to create a new kind of business for a new kind of customer.

In their business model, customers would not buy jets or fractional shares of jets. Instead, customers would buy prepaid cards entitling them to 25 hours of jet time. The cards would range in price from $109,900 to $299,900, depending on the aircraft.

These two innovative entrepreneurs approached NetJets, the largest provider of fractional jet services. NetJets operates one of the most advanced aviation facilities in the world. It maintains a full-time staff of meteorologists and employs 2,800 seasoned pilots, including several former Air Force One captains. NetJets is owned by Warren Buffett's Berkshire Hathaway, Inc. In essence, Kenny and Jesse proposed selling shares of shares in the NetJets fleet, opening up a new and potentially lucrative audience of customers who were priced out of the existing market.

Richard Santulli, NetJets' chairman and CEO, and Jim Jacobs, NetJets' vice chairman, were intrigued. Soon a deal was cut and Marquis Jet Partners was born. Kenny and

BALLS!

Jesse personally sold the first 100 cards. Their early customers included Run-DMC, Jay-Z, and P-Diddy. Their current roster of celebrity clients includes Catherine Zeta-Jones and Kelly Ripa, as well as golfer Jim Furyk, wide receiver Keyshawn Johnson, and basketball star Tracy McGrady.

Ready for Prime Time

As if having Warren Buffett in their corner wasn't enough, the Marquis Jet team got an additional boost from Donald Trump. Marquis Jet was featured on the second episode of *The Apprentice*, Trump's prime-time business reality show. Two rival squads of wannabe-Donalds were handed the task of developing an ad campaign for Marquis Jet.

Ken Austin, the company's executive vice president and chief marketing and business development officer, says giving Trump's contestants the green light to devise an ad campaign while millions of viewers watched was a calculated risk. "We really didn't know what they would come up with," Ken recalls. "But I knew that we needed an ad campaign and I also knew what it would cost if we handed the assignment to a firm here in Manhattan."

As it turned out, Marquis Jet decided not to use the campaign developed on the show. But the exposure itself was enough to double the company's sales leads. Daily traffic at the Marquis web site leaped from 1,500 to 20,000 on the day the episode aired. In an unexpected bonus, Marquis received hundreds of unsolicited proposals for ad campaigns.

The episode proved so popular that Marquis Jet was invited back for prominent roles in three more episodes of *The Apprentice*, including the two-hour season finale.

"*The Apprentice* was a spectacular infomercial for us, in prime time," says Bill Allard, CEO of Marquis Jet. "Participating in the show was a risk worth taking."

Finding the Sweet Spot

Like Who's Calling, Marquis Jet experienced phenomenal growth in its first three years. The company now serves more than 2,000 clients and generates more than $300 million in annual revenue. In 2004, the *Robb Report* included Marquis Jet on its "Best of the Best" list. Marquis Jet also received the Flight International Aerospace Industry Award held in Singapore for great achievements in business/corporate aviation, and *Business Traveler* magazine hailed Marquis for offering the industry's best private jet card program.

Despite their quick climb to the stratosphere, the Marquis team feels driven to provide incomparably superior service to their customers, whom they refer to as "owners."

BALLS!

At Marquis Jet, bravery is a cherished virtue, especially when it's required to fulfill a customer's special or unusual need. The Marquis Jet staff often coordinates car services to bring a client's friends or relatives to the airport. They'll stock up on each child's preferred snack, track down the family canine's dog biscuit, or find a kid-friendly movie on DVD.

"When someone is paying $5,000 or more to fly on their own jet, any issue is a big issue," explains Ken Dichter. "We have to respond immediately, within minutes. All of our customers know they can call us at home—and some really do. They all know we will do whatever it takes to make them happy."

Even after Marquis Jet has satisfied the whims and wants of its pampered clientele, the company's founders and 70 employees remain vigilant. "We can't relax, we can't sit back and we can never be satisfied," says Ken Austin. "We're too passionate about our work here. And to be honest, we're paranoid—in a healthy way. We go to bed every night expecting to read something in tomorrow's *Wall Street Journal* that will turn everything upside down and create a bunch of new opportunities for us."

Speaking of new opportunities, you never know when one is going to bubble to the surface. We'll end our first chapter with a story about a visionary whose business is literally in his blood—and maybe occasionally in yours, too!

Brewing Up a New Business

What a foolish waste of time! That's what his dad thought when Jim Koch formed The Boston Beer Company in 1984. Jim's father, Charles, was a fifth-generation brewer who had left the business decades earlier when the large national brewers began swallowing up small regional breweries across the country. Young Jim Koch had seen his father's disappointment on a daily basis.

Instead of entering the beer business like his father, Jim enrolled at Harvard College, where he earned a bachelor's degree in government. He was the first Koch son in 150 years not to become a brewer.

During a hiatus from his studies, Jim joined Outward Bound as a mountaineering instructor. He spent three years on the mountains before returning to Harvard, where he earned simultaneous graduate degrees in business administration and law. He joined the Boston Consulting Group in 1978 and began a successful six-year career advising the CEOs of Fortune 500 companies on business matters. But eventually the beer business beckoned.

Here's the way Jim describes it in his company bio: "My father went crazy when I told him I wanted to start my own brewery. 'We've spent 20 years trying to get the brew smell out of our clothes,' he said. I eventually came to believe that it wasn't in the clothes, it was in the blood.

BALLS!

My dad shook his head, but at some level, he must have liked the idea, because he became my first investor."

Jim's father listened and finally went up to the attic of the family home to dig out his old beer recipes. He gave a favorite to his son, one that dated back to Jim's great-great-grandfather, Louis Koch, who in the 1870s brewed a beer named Louis Koch Lager at his brewery in St. Louis, Missouri. This recipe became the flagship beer of The Boston Beer Company, Samuel Adams Boston Lager.

With the recipe in hand, Jim began home brewing in his kitchen. He liked what he brewed. It tasted great. His secretary at Boston Consulting Group, Rhonda Kallman, who became Jim's partner and vice president of sales and marketing, liked the beer. Now they needed to sell the beer.

Six-Pack Briefcase

Selling an unknown beer wasn't easy. Beer distributors were completely uninterested in Jim's beer, so he took to the streets. He and Rhonda sold Samuel Adams Boston Lager door-to-door to bartenders and restaurant managers in the Boston area. They believed in their product.

"I had six cold beers in unlabelled bottles and chill packs in my old consulting briefcase," recalls Jim.

"I learned something on the job they never taught me in business school: how to sell. I realized that selling is the heart of any business."

Initially, the idea of selling frightened him. He didn't like selling, but he had no money to hire a sales staff. So he screwed up his courage, put on his best suit, and sold his beer. He remembers the bar manager at one bar looking at him suspiciously before he convinced him to taste the beer. The reaction from the bar manager was an order of 25 cases. Jim knew he needed about 30 accounts to get The Boston Beer Company going. He had only 29 more to go.

The Boston Beer Company Today

Today, The Boston Beer Company, which issued an initial public offering (IPO) in 1995, is the leading craft brewer in the nation. The company is also the sixth largest brewer in the United States, selling about 1.2 million barrels of beer a year.

In 2003, The Boston Beer Company's net income was $10.6 million and the company's net revenue was $207.9 million. It has 280 employees and sells its beers in all 50 states, plus Canada, Asia, Australia, and Europe—20 countries altogether.

There are currently 20 beers in The Boston Beer Com-

BALLS!

pany portfolio, which has won over 650 awards internationally since 1985. In addition to beer, The Boston Beer Company also makes and sells Hard Core ciders and several Twisted Tea products.

The Boston Beer Company has been named by *Boston* magazine as one of the best companies to work for and by *The Princeton Review* as a company with one of the best entry-level jobs. Jim was named an Entrepreneur of the Year by *Inc.* magazine in 1995.

Crucial Innovations

Like the entrepreneurs we've just met, Jim sees innovation as the lifeblood of a successful business.

"You can't succeed without coming up with ways to do things better," says Jim. "It doesn't have to be a new microchip or a new way to surf the Web, but you have to be able to see and do things differently. You need the ability to see things as they really are, as opposed to looking at things as paradigms and ambiguities that confuse you."

A crucial innovation at The Boston Beer Company was how Jim decided to brew his beer—not the actual technical process of brewing, but *where* it was brewed. Jim decided that the company would contract out its brewing.

"The old pathway for starting a small microbrewery," says Jim, "was to find some old, almost broken-down brewing or dairy equipment and bottling line and get some of your buddies together to learn how to weld and build a brewery. I found that model an unacceptable way to make beer, especially if you have any respect for quality."

Jim spent a week in 1983 working at one of the first microbreweries on the East Coast, now long out of business. It was his experience there that convinced him *not* to build his own brewery. "You only occasionally get a good batch of beer this way," says Jim. "Too often you get bad, infected beer."

This was unacceptable for Jim. "My mission was to make great beer, every time. I knew that there were established regional breweries in the country that had world-class quality standards and excess capacity where I could contract space and make my beer from my recipe."

Jim believes that the reason for The Boston Beer Company's success is consistency. "It was the first craft beer to which consumers could be brand loyal because they knew that every glass would taste the same and taste great," says Jim.

Jim did eventually purchase two breweries, one in Boston and one in Cincinnati, but only after he was certain they could maintain the highest standards of quality

BALLS!

from batch to batch. Those two breweries account for about half the company's beer. The rest is still brewed under the contract system Jim envisioned when he started up the company.

The Best Days

Jim says that one of the two best days of his life at The Boston Beer Company was April 8, 1985. "That was the day I tasted the first absolutely perfect batch of Samuel Adams Boston Lager," recalls Jim. "Before then, I had home brewed in my kitchen and then brewed a batch at the facilities at the University of California, Davis (a university widely praised for its wine and beer fermentation program). This first perfect batch was brewed at Pittsburgh Brewing."

Jim adds, "I remember saying, 'Wow! This is really great beer and something good is going to happen.'"

His other great day came two months later in Colorado at the Great American Beer Festival (GABF), the largest and most prestigious consumer beer festival in the United States. Samuel Adams Boston Lager won first prize in the Consumer Preference Poll at the festival. Best of all, Jim's father was right there.

"My dad had flown to the festival to help me pour the

beer. When it was announced we had won, hundreds of people started to flock to our table to taste my family's beer. I caught a glimpse of my father, who was literally being swept aside by the crowd. He was standing there, just shaking his head and smiling."

Long Shot World Homebrew Contest

Twenty years ago, "the line between microbrewing and home brewing was almost invisible," says Jim. Since then, a chasm has opened between professional craft brewers and the home brewers. Jim feels that's a shame, because each community of brewers has knowledge to offer the other.

In 1996 and 1997, The Boston Beer Company sponsored the Long Shot World Homebrew Contest. Jim's idea was to search for the best home brews in three beer style categories, brew them professionally, and distribute them.

The name "Long Shot" came to Jim and his brewers as they looked at the cooler where the first year's entries were stored. They realized what a long shot it would be for a home brewer to have a beer that he or she probably made in the kitchen distributed nationally.

The contest was a perfect marriage of skills, recalls Jim. It combined home brewing knowledge with Jim's ability to take an original recipe brewed in someone's home, reproduce it faithfully in a larger facility, and then

BALLS!

bring it to market. The contest also served as a vivid reminder of the company's roots in home brewing.

Liquid Lunches

In 2000 Jim launched a 10-city Liquid Lunch tour in which he pitted Samuel Adams beers against similar-style European beers. Three Samuel Adams beers and two locally crafted brews were matched one-on-one at each tasting against popular leading imported beers that were the same in style and class—lagers with lagers, pale ales with pale ales, and so on.

Jim began each Liquid Lunch session with a quick lesson on the basics of tasting good beer. He used rating forms and procedures developed by the American Homebrewers Association, in which the beers were scored according to appearance, aroma, flavor, mouth feel, and overall impression.

The Liquid Lunch tour, which took place during National Beer Month (also supported by The Boston Beer Company) was designed by Jim to "educate and enlighten beer drinkers about the wonders of fresh, well-made American beer." Tour cities included Philadelphia, Minneapolis, Denver, San Diego, Los Angeles, San Francisco, New York, Atlanta, Baltimore, and Boston.

In 30 different blind taste tests, Samuel Adams came up the winner. But the real winner was The Boston Beer Company, which created a reservoir of goodwill for itself without spending a ton of money.

I'm impressed with the variety of ideas Jim came up with to promote his vision. I'm impressed that he was brave enough to act on them. I believe that Jim's success in business is based on his philosophy of picking a trail to blaze and then adopting the straightforward strategies to blaze that trail. As he says, "Getting to the top of a mountain is a simple undertaking. Brewing beer has a similar kind of simplicity."

I'll drink to that!

Snag the Ideas!

Lonnie Benson loves to find good ideas and products and then make them even better. He isn't afraid to compete against larger or more established opponents, especially after he's identified their vulnerabilities. Here are some ideas for identifying and seizing new opportunities:

❶ *Take a quick survey of your local market.*
See which businesses do the worst job of providing service to their customers. Find out which businesses in your

BALLS!

market charge their customers the most while offering the least. Think of a creative way to cut costs without sacrificing quality. Decide which of the competition's customers are most likely to defect, and make them an offer they can't refuse.

❷ *Look outside your comfort zone for ideas.*
Every month, Lonnie forces himself to read numerous publications that cover industries he isn't familiar with. He gets some of his best ideas from articles that have absolutely nothing to do with sales, marketing, or telecommunications.

❸ *Make a list of local businesses that everyone talks about.*
These are the guys you want to compete against or partner with. They obviously have a market for what they sell since they have enough customers to generate a buzz! Figure out a way to take better care of those customers at a reasonable price. Or find a way you can complement their business.

❹ *Never stay discouraged.*
Everyone else gets discouraged and that's why so many people never actually start new ventures. Don't be afraid to compete and to fail. You can't win unless you're willing to play the game and lose once in a while. Learn from every mistake. Lonnie has started several businesses that went nowhere. A friend of ours, Chase Fraser, had an

idea for a company that specialized in innovative survey and e-mail marketing campaigns. When he first started raising money for his new company, the first person he pitched was Mark Serif, one of the co-founders of America Online (AOL). Understandably, he was nervous. He went through the pitch, and Mark listened patiently—and then shot his idea full of holes. "I left the meeting very dejected, and for the briefest of moments, I felt like throwing in the towel," says Chase. "Instead, I went home, learned from what I did wrong the first time, improved my approach, and made my second pitch a few days later—then my third and fourth. Eventually, the original failed pitch resulted in attracting capital from nine investors. Today my company, MarketQuiz, isn't just a dream—it's a reality."

Remember this: When you start hitting home runs, everyone forgets about the times you struck out. They talk about your .350 batting average, not your 650 strikeouts. Look at each strikeout or failure as bringing you one step closer to a home run.

BALLS!

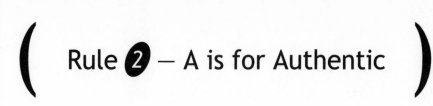

Rule **2** — A is for Authentic

Rule ② — A is for Authentic

A long time ago, I would play Scrabble with a neighborhood kid who always made up big words. He bluffed his way through game after game until someone finally whipped out a dictionary and tripped him up.

Sometimes I think of that guy when I meet people at trade shows and business events who act as if they're still living in the dot-com days. What amazes me is that they expect you to fall for their hype. Don't they know that their bluff has been called? The giddy era of easy money is over. It's dead and gone.

The smart people I know have acquired a taste for old-fashioned business values—with a twist. They've discovered there are tried-and-true business practices that you simply can't ignore if you want to play the game and play it well.

Today's successful entrepreneur is more like a farmer than a big-game hunter. Today's entrepreneur understands that all companies, large and small, follow natural cycles. There's an inevitable rhythm to the business process that cannot be disregarded.

In other words, we all have experienced a return to reality. We realize now that being intelligent is better than being clever, that being honest is better than being smooth, and that being authentic is better than being slick.

Authentic means being real, embracing the business world for what it is and not trying to gloss over the challenges, risks, and dangers we face in today's global economy. Authentic means remembering that business is mostly about hard work, discipline, the willingness to accept disappointment, and the strength to learn from failure.

If that sounds awfully old-fashioned, I plead guilty. But hey, I'm still playing Scrabble—and I don't have to make up big words to win. Sometimes KISS—keep it simple, stupid—is simply smart.

("Many people fail simply because they conclude that **fundamentals** simply do not apply in their case.")

~ M.L. Cichon

BALLS!

Show Me the Return

I want what John F. Stapleton has: experience, success, and money, plus the freedom and the time to do whatever he wants. Come to think of it, a lot of people I know want what John has. John is our CEO, and right now he is leading the charge at Who's Calling.

John doesn't *look* like a guy who doesn't need to work. He won't talk about his different homes unless you bring them up. He doesn't brag about his past success—in fact, you have to practically beg him to tell you about it. And when he does talk about it he says he has learned more from his failures than from his successes. He rarely wears a suit, he doesn't fly around in his own plane, and he certainly doesn't charter yachts for around-the-world cruises. But if you look carefully, you can tell he has many, many stories to tell, and the Irish twinkle in his eye lets you know some of them are pretty wild.

John is a fatherly figure, the kind who doles out strange proverbial bits of sage advice such as, "The one-eyed man is king in the valley of the blind," and, "There's a pony somewhere in all this poop—we just have to find it." John's willingness to share his knowledge and experience with his colleagues, the value he places on the people around him, his disciplined approach to business, and his direct, self-assured mannerisms—plus the fact that you never know when he is going to jump on one of his many motorcycles to race Lonnie across town—set the tone for life at Who's Calling. He doesn't have an executive jet, but he probably should. Since joining our team, John has spent every Monday morning flying from his home in Minneapolis to our office in Seattle. He has a condo on Lake Washington, though he might as well sleep at the office during the week. At the end of each week he flies back to his incredibly understanding and generous wife, Mary.

"Life's too short for not enjoying yourself and enjoying your work," says John. "For me they are one and the same. My companies become my family."

He also believes that life's too short for head games and ego trips. "Successful businesses encourage collaboration and teamwork," he says. "You need to trust the people you work with and they need to trust you."

When John says that "trust is the foundation of our business," he's not just blowing smoke. He means it. From John's perspective, trust is the necessary prerequisite for discipline, and discipline is the necessary prerequisite for making a profit.

"You can hire a bunch of salespeople and begin generating revenue. That's easy," he says. "The hard part is creating the discipline required to earn respectable profits consistently, over time. Revenue is nice, but it must produce a profit."

BALLS!

A Day at the Courthouse

John wasn't always our CEO. And we weren't always profitable before John. If you were wondering how a stern but fatherly guy like John found himself in cahoots with a blue-sky visionary like Lonnie, the answer is simple: It all began with a lawsuit.

Long before Who's Calling, one of John's companies sued one of Lonnie's companies. Then Lonnie sued back. Things were getting ugly. John remembers it well:

"I walked into the required settlement conference before getting to the courthouse and saw all those lawyers in their fancy suits, carrying expensive briefcases. I counted up the lawyers and did a few expense calculations in my head. It didn't take me long to realize that it would be crazy for me and Lonnie to fight a court battle. We'd both wind up losing a bunch of money, and the lawyers on both sides would have a field day. So I took Lonnie aside and we talked. And we talked. And we talked. . . ."

By the end of their conversation, both men had agreed to drop their lawsuits. Even more important than that, Lonnie realized that he had just made a new friend—a friend he could trust, even under the most difficult circumstances. A few years later, Lonnie asked John to run Who's Calling.

Here's John's perspective on their *Odd Couple* relationship: "I bring something to the table that Lonnie, God bless him, doesn't have in great abundance—discipline. On the other hand, I don't have Lonnie's natural instinct for developing new products. Our strengths are complementary and we trust each other to do what's right for the company."

Cash Flow, Cash Flow, Cash Flow

Like Lonnie, John emerged from modest roots. He grew up in Brooklyn, an ordinary kid in an ordinary neighborhood. His gift for peddling and his willingness to work long hours enabled him to support a small family. He worked in a variety of sales roles until one day, he simply got tired of following someone else's lead. He wanted to run things his way, and in the early 1970s, he got his chance to start his own company. A client of his offered to give John his business if John could do a better job than the current vendor.

After becoming his own boss, John never looked back. He has started up or turned around dozens of firms. He has invested in many more. Over the years, he has learned to see past the sizzle when he sizes up a company.

"I look at three things—cash flow, cash flow, cash flow. The single most common mistake that people make

BALLS!

when trying to run a small business is ignoring cash flow," says John.

"I look at the cash flow of Who's Calling at 2 P.M. every day, rain or shine. I look at cash flow the way a doctor looks at blood pressure—it's a vital sign, a window into a hidden world. Cash flow is a critical indicator of our company's health and well-being. Cash flow tells me when I've got to take corrective action, such as reducing or delaying expenditures. Cash flow tells me if our revenue plan is on track or heading off the rails. Cash flow validates our assumptions, or proves them wrong. Cash flow is the ultimate reality—and yet it's so basic."

If cash flow is so basic, then why do many companies play fast and loose with it? "In most cases, it's a lack of discipline and a lack of common sense. Sometimes it's a lack of simple business knowledge," says John.

"Many businesspeople, believe it or not, confuse expense with expenditure. When they buy a new computer for $3,000, their accountant tells them they can depreciate it over three years. So they're going to record an expense of $1,000 per year for the new computer. In the first year, the remaining $2,000 temporarily disappears—from an accounting perspective. But from a cash flow perspective, $3,000 has gone out."

John's adamant refusal to play accounting games explains our healthy cash flow at Who's Calling. It's also one of the reasons I consider him an authentic businessperson. He's the real McCoy, not a fictional millionaire marooned on a deserted island with a bunch of castaways.

Model Maker

One of John's first tasks at Who's Calling was to rein in our spending. He also recruited a skilled chief operating officer, Stuart DePina. Stuart was the chief financial officer who guided the successful IPO of TicketMaster, and we're thrilled to now have him on our team.

When John arrived at Who's Calling, we were like many young companies: totally focused on signing up new clients, at any cost. Without even trying, our cost of sales had skyrocketed to 42 cents on the dollar!

"That was completely unacceptable," says John. "How can you ever hope to make a profit if you're giving away the first 42 cents of every dollar you take in? Your chances are slim to none, and I've got bad news for you: Slim just left town."

John's experience soon inspired a solution. It wouldn't be easy, it wouldn't be quick, and it wouldn't be painless. But it would work.

BALLS!

"When I first got here, they were doing a rough calculation at the end of every month to estimate the cost of sales. That's not my idea of discipline. To be fair, it's easier for a company that manufactures a tangible product to calculate its cost of sales than it is for us. But the mere fact that we sell intangible services doesn't let us off the hook."

John had two choices: He could build a cost accounting system that would keep track of every expenditure down to the last paper clip. Or he could build a model that would establish an understanding of all costs involved in delivering a sale, including sales costs.

"Cost accounting systems are great for huge companies like Boeing. But for a company of our size, they don't make a lot of sense. I'd rather build a model, test it, and tinker with it until it's running smoothly."

In practice, John's model works like this: Before we sell a service, we calculate all the real and potential costs associated with providing the service. If our costs seem likely to exceed 20 percent of the dollar value of the sale, the deal might be off. If they exceed 30 percent, the deal is definitely off. If that seems too greedy, remember that John's 20 percent target covers only our costs to provide the service. It

doesn't include the costs of marketing, sales, administration, finance, research and development (R&D), and the like. Those costs typically chew up another 50 to 60 percent of the revenue dollar, leaving a pretax profit of between 20 and 30 percent. We now build all of our budgets with this understanding.

"We still do a lot of guesstimating to figure out how much client service time goes into an account that bills $1,000 a month," explains John. "It's frustrating, but it's not unusual for a company our size. Being innovative adds another dimension of uncertainty to the equation. We're constantly introducing new products to stay three or four steps ahead of the competition. That makes it difficult to nail down our costs with total accuracy."

Because costs tend to be a moving target, John continually sharpens the model, testing it against results and recalibrating often. "You must test your assumptions in the real world to find out whether they're right or wrong. There's no embarrassment in being wrong—as long as you find out quickly enough to do something about it!"

Flashing Lights and Sirens

True to his instincts, John also targeted our product management model. He restructured our management team,

BALLS!

creating a new model that starts with an in-depth understanding of how our clients use our products, and looks at ways we can continually bring more value to the table. John insisted that we focus on becoming an integral part of our clients' business practices. He also recognized that we needed to develop closer and deeper relationships with our existing clients, rather than devoting most of our energy to hunting down new clients. By learning more about our existing clients, we could anticipate their real needs more effectively.

Here's an example of how John's focused approach to business made a big difference: One of our top products is a service called Voice View. It's a real-time, interactive system that records a client's inbound calls and then makes them available for review over the Internet or by phone without any special hardware or software. Voice View also has a "Whisper" feature that lets whoever answers the call know which promotion or advertisement prompted the call—before they are connected with the caller!

Voice View also automatically matches inbound phone numbers with individual caller names and addresses—and it provides all of this information in a real-time lead management interface on the World Wide Web. But providing this name and address match feature requires us to contract with two other companies to get the most updated name and address matches for each number. Here's where things start getting interesting.

When Who's Calling launched this feature, John's predecessors assumed that having superior automatic matching capabilities would create a competitive advantage for the service. And even though they knew that offering the best matching rates in the country, in real time, would increase the cost of our product, they decided it was worth the additional expense—and the reduced margins.

At John's urging, we took a closer look at all of our products and services. We asked ourselves: Are they providing true value to our clients? What business problems are they solving? Are they *cost effective?* We discovered that very few of our clients were actually using our automatic name and address matching feature on a daily basis. *We* were proud of it and *we* thought it was really cool, but our customers didn't seem to care very much about it unless they were sending out a targeted direct mail campaign. That was a revelation.

We also looked carefully at our cost structure and saw that when we automatically matched for every client, the cost of goods rose dramatically. When we saw that, it was the equivalent of seeing flashing red lights and hearing loud sirens. More important, our clients didn't know all the uses for the product, and therefore they were not getting the full value.

BALLS!

Now we've found a way to do automatic matching only when our clients need it while giving them "best practice" tips and advice on how and why they should use it. We've also started conducting Monthly Account Reviews (MARs) with our clients, to illuminate their business problems with the data that we generate from the phone lead. This is how we help focus our client on their business challenges and solve their problems more effectively. It also differentiates us from the competition. We regularly work with our clients, finding new ways for them to use our services and to improve their sales and marketing processes.

By taking on more of a consulting role, we build tighter relationships with our clients. We're able to introduce new products and services that ease the business pains our clients feel. Our products are still cool, but now they address larger and more complex business problems. It's a win for us and a big win for our clients.

"We can do *anything* we want, but we can't do *everything* we want," John often says. "Without first taking the time to understand how we can bring added value, we were simply throwing mud at the wall and hoping some of it would stick. Luckily we've been willing to learn from past models of success, like General Mills. We used

to sell our clients flour and hope they would make a cake. Now we not only sell them the cake mix, we'll even bake it for them!"

Without John's experience and model, it would have been difficult to know where to begin tackling the problem. The good news is that by applying the model, we not only saved money, but we made ourselves more competitive over the long term and our clients get real value from our services. And yes, we still check our cash flow pulse and we've got a strong, steady beat.

Trial and Error

There's no West Point for business leaders, and even an MBA from Harvard Business School can't guarantee success. If there's any single point of agreement among the men and women I've interviewed for this book, it's that success in business is almost always the result of trial and error.

For any of you seeking a shortcut to riches or a quick path to glory, this will come as bad news. The trial and error approach invariably requires heavy doses of patience, endurance, self-confidence, and the ability to accept occasional failure. The winners in this book weren't *born* winners—they *became* winners because they didn't surrender, they learned from their mistakes, and they kept their eyes wide open.

BALLS!

Brad Miller, the CEO of Perimeter Internetworking in Trumbull, Connecticut, is creative and disciplined. He's just the right guy to guide a small company through the twists and turns of today's savagely competitive business environment.

Perimeter Internetworking provides managed information technology (IT) services, such as wide area network (WAN), Internet protocol (IP) telephony, e-mail, and Internet security. Perimeter's financial backers recruited Brad in 2000, after concluding that the firm's original business model wasn't working.

"Most of our prospects already had a WAN, e-mail, and some kind of security system in place," recalls Brad. "They'd already made their investments and there's typically a five-year replacement cycle. So if we didn't arrive at the 'magic moment' when they were ready to replace one of their systems, we were out of luck."

Brad realized that the company didn't have time to sell products with long sales cycles. "I knew we couldn't afford to waste our energy trying to guess when someone would need a new WAN. That meant we needed to focus on products that didn't require finding the 'magic moment' to make a sale." That required a big shift and a lot of focus.

Brad decided to narrow the company's marketing efforts to concentrate on one service—network security.

Then he went a step further, focusing Perimeter's attention squarely on one market—community banks.

"We focused on network security for community banks because banks are required by federal law to overcome their security challenges. And unlike other federal regulations, the banking laws are strictly enforced. So if a bank doesn't stay on top of its network security challenges, it's in big trouble."

The other attractive aspect about the community banking market is its receptivity to outsourcing. "Most community financial institutions already outsource their IT needs, so they require less missionary work on our part to convince them that outsourcing is a good idea," says Brad. "You can't spend all your time in front of the client evangelizing and preaching basic concepts. Sometimes it's necessary, but mostly it's a waste of energy."

By sharpening its focus and emphasizing its expertise in security, Perimeter was able to stand out from the crowd of managed service providers. "Network security gets us in the door, but it's not profitable enough on its own. That's why we didn't get rid of our portfolio of additional services—we just shifted them into the background from a marketing perspective," explains Brad.

"After we develop a level of trust with the customer, we try to sell as many of our other services as possible."

BALLS!

Brad's three-pronged strategy of

 simplifying the marketing message,

reducing the initial choice of products, and

choosing a receptive audience

has paid off handsomely.

While the clients of competitors produce average monthly revenue of less than $1,000, Perimeter's clients generate average monthly revenue in excess of $5,000. "Our ability to sell additional services has been absolutely critical to our success. First we get our toe in the door, followed by our foot, ankle, shin, knee, and thigh."

Wanted: 100 Geniuses

Andy Greenawalt, the founder of Perimeter's parent firm, reminds me of Lonnie Benson. Each is an entrepreneurial wizard, visionary techie, and modern-day Renaissance man.

Both are fortunate to have linked up with experienced business partners with the ability to convert their brilliance into a steady stream of commercial successes. For Lonnie, that business partner is John Stapleton. For Andy, it's Brad Miller.

"Andy could go into any sales meeting and always wind up selling someone something," recalls Brad. "He has the intelligence, the charisma, and the energy to make things happen. But then again, he has an IQ of 150. We needed a business model that didn't require us to hire 100 geniuses like Andy to make sales."

In its early days, Andy's company had tried to follow the examples set by other managed service firms. Those firms—most of which have since failed—hired flashy sales execs, and gave them lavish expense accounts and huge commissions. They tried to be all things to all people, hoping that the ever-increasing demand for new technology would carry them along.

"Our company's cost of sales went through the roof because we had hired stars from huge companies who didn't understand the realities of growing a small business," says Brad.

One of Brad's first tasks at Perimeter was reining in the sales force and recalibrating its approach to the market. "The priority shouldn't be to grow as fast as you can. The priority should be to find out what works and what doesn't. To me this is common sense. Test your ideas first in a small market. Then go out and hire a bunch of people and replicate your success."

Resisting pressure from the investors who had hired him, Brad spent most of 2001 testing his assumptions about the market. In 2002, he hired two more sales reps, again resisting pressure from investors who wanted him to add staff more quickly. At the beginning of 2003, he decided the company needed a new sales process and began rewriting the sales playbook.

By the end of 2003, he was satisfied that Perimeter had the right sales processes in place. "That's when we really started hiring," he says. "There were no shortcuts. We found the right path through trial and error."

Many companies sabotage themselves by skipping critical steps in the trial and error process. Rushing the process might save time, but you won't absorb the knowledge you need to make crucial management decisions.

Test, Test, Test

"Can you imagine a Fortune 500 company launching a new product or service without testing it thoroughly? If big companies like IBM and McDonald's test their products, why can't smaller companies?"

Brad enjoys posing questions like these. He widens his eyes and waves his hands to emphasize his amazement.

"For some reason, many start-ups don't like to test. They think it's a waste of time. Or a sign of weakness. But they're wrong. Just because someone is willing to invest capital in you doesn't mean you're ready for prime time. You have to test your assumptions in the real world and make sure you are not wasting your precious funds on an inefficient sales process," says Brad. "Test, test, test." Sounds like test, test, test might just equate to cash flow, cash flow, cash flow.

For example, many technology companies assume that when they reach a certain size, they need a national sales force with fancy offices in major cities, a generous travel budget, and the freedom to roam endlessly in pursuit of big-name clients. This assumption is both false and dangerous, says Brad.

"Building a remote sales force is a major challenge for any company selling a complex product. It's one thing for the company founder to be pitching a highly sophisticated software product that he helped design. It's an entirely different thing for a sales rep living 3,000 miles away to be pitching the same product," says Brad. "One of the painful lessons we learned was that we couldn't allow our sales force in the field to define the sales process. That's a sure recipe for unhappiness and disaster."

Perimeter also discovered that its sales reps could not serve as credible product experts—the product was just

BALLS!

too complicated for any single rep to master. The sales team was very good, though, at setting the stage for complex pitches from Andy or some of their other technical experts.

"So we encouraged the sales reps to see themselves as movie directors or orchestra conductors, instead of trying to act like technology gurus. It worked fine and everyone was happy," Brad recalls. "That's the advantage of staying close to the sales process—you can fix something when it's not working."

Using his common sense philosophy, Brad has grown the company's top line impressively. Perimeter has won multiple awards for sales growth, including the 2004 Connecticut Deloitte Technology Fast 50, the 2004 North America Technology Fast 500, as well as the Connecticut Innovations Sales Growth Award in both 2003 and 2001. More important, Perimeter has been profitable every month since December 2001. And its annual sales revenue has grown from $500,000 to more than $16 million in just five years.

With less than $4.5 million in invested capital in 2004, Perimeter is roughly 10 times more efficient per dollar of invested capital than its competitors. Each of Perimeter's 50 employees generates average annual revenues of more than $300,000—making them over three times more efficient than their counterparts at competing organizations.

"Top management must be in the trenches with the sales force to understand the forces driving customers to make purchase decisions," says Brad. "You can't sit in an ivory tower and issue commands. You've got to listen and learn. And test."

The Guru of Flavor

Let's take a break from the tech guys and visit Leanna Mix of Da Vinci Gourmet. First of all, anyone with the last name Mix who is the beverage development manager at a successful gourmet coffee syrup company located in Seattle simply *has* to be the real deal. Da Vinci Gourmet creates, manufactures, and markets gourmet syrups, tea concentrates, and gourmet sauces in 54 countries. The company's unique line of 140 flavored syrups includes German Chocolate Cake, Peppermint Patty, Dutch Apple Pie, Blue Curaçao, Guava, Huckleberry, Kiwi, Passion Fruit, and Tiramisu.

The company's co-founders, Greg Davenport and Bill Cotter, were noted for their pursuit of perfect flavors, perfect colors, and perfect textures in their products. The endless quest for perfection is reflected by the company's reputation, the pride of its workforce, and its steady growth in earnings. After starting the business with a small cash investment in 1989, they recently sold the company to The Kerry Group, an international maker of food ingredients based in Tralee, Ireland. The original and authentic spirit of Davenport and Cotter is evident throughout the company's 66,000-square-foot facility in South Seattle.

Leanna's work involves travel, tasting, and remembering. Her trained palate and her expertise as a marketer are crucial to maintaining Da Vinci's global reputation for offering flavors that are absolutely authentic. "I'm a foodie at heart, but I combine that with my knowledge of marketing to create opportunities for our clients to profit," Leanna explains.

Part of Leanna's job requires her to assume the pose of an international bar-hopper, tasting novel concoctions whenever and wherever they appear and watching for trends even before they start. "My rule is to never take more than two sips," she declares.

London, she says, is the unofficial capital of cocktails. "They use unexpected ingredients such as fresh ground pepper and gingerroot in their drinks. Very unusual!" she says. Based on her observations, Leanna predicts that the black pepper pineapple mojito, a rum-based cocktail that traces its roots back to Cuba, will become in-

creasingly popular among Americans seeking authentic foreign drinks.

One of the company's larger clients is Borders, which uses Da Vinci Gourmet syrups to flavor the drinks served at its in-store coffee bars. Leanna noticed that during the Halloween season, one of the large national candy makers markets a lollipop that tastes like a caramel apple. She knew the Green Apple smoothie was already a popular drink at Borders. She suggested combining it with Da Vinci's caramel syrup to create a Caramel Apple smoothie.

The drink became wildly popular, validating Leanna's creative instinct. Best of all, it required no additional spending by Borders, since the key ingredients were already on its shelves.

"This isn't rocket science. It's more a matter of not pushing the envelope too far," she says. For example, one of the more popular mocha drinks is a Snickers mocha, which essentially combines two instantly recognizable flavors.

"People enjoy tasting flavors that are unique and familiar at the same time," says Leanna. "Combinations of flavors can invoke pleasant memories of the past, creating enjoyable experiences. Flavors can also trigger emotions that make people feel good."

BALLS!

For Leanna and her colleagues at Da Vinci Gourmet, staying authentic often means saying no. "If you have a client who wants to serve a drink made with Indonesian cinnamon, miniature bananas, and fresh lychee nuts, then you have to tell him it's a tad too exotic for his menu."

Sometimes a client will request a flavor combination that just won't work, such as black pepper pineapple coffee. That's when Leanna has to be firm, diplomatic, and inventive. One large client wanted its coffee bars to serve Thai coffee, which is made with a special kind of chicory-tinged coffee, ground cardamom, coriander, and sweet condensed milk. The main ingredients are expensive and "polarizing," which is the food industry's polite way of saying "people will either love it or hate it."

"We asked the client's team to describe what they actually liked about Thai coffee. They said it was sweet, it was spicy, and it was easy to make. Based on that description, we came up with a new syrup that could be simply added to coffee and milk. The drink had a flavor profile that was similar to Thai coffee, but was less polarizing."

Da Vinci won't just say no to a single client. Instead they look for ways to maintain their brand and profit margins while still coming up with inventive products their clients can sell. For years, the company refused to make sugar-free syrups, believing the available artificial sweeteners would alter the taste and texture of its products. It

wasn't until the introduction of Splenda that Da Vinci found a sugar substitute that satisfied its rigorous standards. Now Da Vinci offers a line of sugar-free flavors that includes Blueberry, Butter Rum, Amaretto, and Crème de Menthe.

The decision to delay its entry into the sugar-free category undoubtedly cost the company some of its market share but ultimately paid off by maintaining its high standard of quality. Da Vinci Gourmet makes no apologies. At Da Vinci Gourmet, authenticity is a core competency.

"We're known for making quality products that make people happy," says Leanna. "We create pleasurable experiences for millions of people, all over the world." And they're going to continue to deliver quality and good taste for years to come.

Snag the Ideas!

John Stapleton has launched dozens of new businesses and saved dozens more. If you're starting up your own business or just looking for a few innovative ways to keep your business authentic, here are some good ideas to snag:

❶ *Don't hide your vision and values.*
Too many businesses hide their vision statement in the annual business plan where you can be sure no one will

BALLS!

read them. Instead make them a part of everyone's regular workday and always keep them short. We put our vision statement on the back of our employee key cards. We also include our values in employee performance reviews and awards. Our values are displayed prominently at employee appreciation events. We create amusing visual aids and memorable graphic devices to ensure that our corporate vision and values are more than just words on a piece of paper. We randomly test each other in meetings and give out prizes to the first person who can repeat our vision: "We revolutionize the sales experience. We are the power behind the sale and the reality behind the experience."

❷ *Measure performance and reward good work on an ongoing basis.*

Provide regular coaching and training to ensure high levels of performance across the organization. Bill Krouse of Polar Chevrolet Mazda records and frequently monitors his dealership's inbound calls so his managers can identify behaviors that generate positive results. He can respond immediately to issues before they become problems. Recording inbound calls and taking the time to review them carefully will enable a committed manager and his or her staff to optimize the value of telephone leads. Playing actual examples of successful and unsuccessful sales calls at meetings is an excellent training tool that can be used to help build scripts for role-playing, as well as to boost employee morale.

❸ Rate quality and set specific goals.

Many successful customer-facing organizations rate the quality of their interactions with customers and set performance goals for their customer service reps. By establishing criteria for effective calls, managers can create a scorecard for each rep, showing appointments made, e-mails received, and other data. With these performance metrics readily available, each employee can quickly see how well he or she is doing. Creating incentives to reward improved performance will quickly establish new norms at higher levels.

❹ Reward and recognize company-wide goals.

Consider setting company-wide goals based on benchmark performance information and your authentic business practices. Integrated measurement and management tools enable businesses to identify areas of strength as well as areas that need more focus. Investigate cost-effective technologies that provide "dashboard" reports, enabling managers to identify and reward positive performance quickly and meaningfully. Invest in a corporate newsletter or intranet so you can easily recognize employees who achieve or exceed the standards you set. Often simple recognition is more valued than money or gifts. A simple phone call or literally a quick visit from a senior manager can make a world of difference.

BALLS!

 Rule ③ — L is for Loud

Rule ❸ — L is for Loud

Be loud. Be heard. Break through the noise of our world's never-ending sales pitch. You're brave. You know to watch the bottom line. Now get noticed.

("Any man who wants to **lead** an orchestra must turn his back on the crowd."

~ James Crook)

Go Big or Stay Home

Here's where I get to talk about my own experiences as a marketer and a corporate executive. Like everyone else in this book, I'm still learning and I don't pretend to have all the answers. Instead of offering advice, I'll share some of my experiences—and you can decide if you want to adopt some of the ways we have jumped way out of the box.

My "date with destiny" began in August 2000, when our next-door neighbor knocked on the door and asked if he could chat. Knowing that I managed ballpark marketing for the Seattle Mariners, he asked me if I had time between home games and batting practices to help him market a new company that had invented a bunch of cool products that would change the way everyone does business. My neighbor was the president of Who's Calling—this was three years before John Stapleton arrived, of course—and what he told me made just enough sense to excite my interest.

Back then, Who's Calling had no marketing plan, no marketing department, and no marketing budget. Its marketing activities consisted largely of photocopied flyers and faxes cooked up by a variety of salespeople as they were running out the door to cold-call whoever would talk to them.

Before I knew it, the die was cast. I met Lonnie, I helped them design a logo, and I was intrigued that with just a little money in the bank, Lonnie decided to bet it all and exhibit at the National Automobile Dealers Association's annual convention in Las Vegas.

If you haven't been to a NADA convention, you haven't tasted fear. Seventeen thousand car dealers and their significant others descend upon the host city like a pack of lions—and they are all King of the Jungle. For four days they own the city and they take no prisoners.

The centerpiece of the annual NADA convention is a trade show—one of the loudest, rowdiest, toughest, and

BALLS!

most competitive trade shows in the world. Naturally, every company in the universe with products or services even remotely related to the automotive industry attends the convention, hoping the trade show floor will somehow magically transform itself into an arena of conquest for their sales forces.

Attracting the wandering eyes of car and truck dealers in this type of festive atmosphere—and holding their attention long enough to make a sale—is a challenge of truly epic proportions. Dealers have notoriously short attention spans, and they are such good salespeople that they will eat you alive if they smell an ounce of fear.

My assignment was simple: put Who's Calling on the map and get our sales team in front of as many automotive dealers as possible. Our team believed they had the balls to sell them and sell them fast. If we didn't make money at the show, we wouldn't be able to make payroll just a few short months later. We had to be big or not come home. So I decided to give the dealers balls, too. And not just any balls. Blue balls.

Twenty Thousand Bucks' Worth of Balls

Twenty thousand dollars. Yes, I really *did* spend $20,000 on little rubber balls with tiny red lights inside that flash when you bounce them.

Maybe I had balls on my mind because I was still working for the Seattle Mariners. The Mariners buy baseballs and fan giveaways the way Starbucks buys coffee beans—in crazy bulk quantities. Some of the balls are actually used by the players during games. But often we just gave the balls away as promotions. Let's face it; they're a much more effective tool for spreading goodwill than brochures or posters. After all, who in their right mind is going to throw away a nice new baseball? Naturally, the team's balls are emblazoned with the Mariners' logo. It's literally a perfect example of hardball marketing.

I'd exhibited at more than my fair share of trade shows through my many past lives at a number of companies, working in both sales and marketing. I knew that you needed a gimmicky giveaway that would be different enough to get them to stop at your booth—something interesting enough to get them to cross onto your patch of carpet. And if you wanted them to remember you after they had recovered from their trade show hangovers, it had to be small enough for them to easily pack home in their overstuffed luggage filled with random brochures and casino smoke filled clothes.

Obviously, the giveaway had to somehow represent our newly formed brand. And that's when I found them, our balls, buried on the inside page of a cluttered promotional catalog. They were round and blue—just like the little illustrated balls in our brand-new logo. They blinked

BALLS!

when you bounced them. We could throw 10,000 of them at people without hurting them (maybe not all at once). And they were just large enough to put a toll-free number on them, just like the vans, so we'd know if they actually generated calls long after the show, enabling us gather an incredible list of prospects.

I loaded up each Who's Calling sales rep with as many of those little blinking balls as they could carry in their pockets. In fact, we recruited nonsalespeople to work the event, since at the time we simply didn't have enough people to fill up the large exhibit booth I had rented. I made up imaginary names for the badges. Dan Horton ended up with the name Richard Smith. Whenever a prospect passed by the Who's Calling booth, "Richard" and the sales reps would begin bouncing the balls. The balls would blink, and as if by magic, every dealer would stop and ask if he could have a ball. While the prospect bounced the ball, the rep pitched. Invariably, the dealer would ask for another two or three balls, depending usually on how many children he said he had.

To make a long story short, our blinking blue balls were the smash hit of the NADA convention. "Richard" sold products that Dan hadn't built yet. Lonnie became the master of the balls and could launch one from 40 feet away and strike within inches of his target. We gave away all 10,000 of them. We were still getting calls for our balls six months after the show.

Most important, the sales force sold more than $400,000 worth of business in just four days, more than all the sales they'd done in the entire previous year of business. By the time we reached our fourth NADA show, we were selling more than $1 million in revenue. My freelance marketing assignment turned into a full-time job, and the rest, as they say, is history.

Since then, I've spent nearly a quarter of a million dollars on blinking blue balls. I can state categorically and undeniably that the phenomenal success of Who's Calling depends largely on its balls—and on our ability to track their performance.

Order Off The Menu
Today, Who's Calling has a real marketing department staffed with wonderful, truly creative people. But our basic approach hasn't changed—we still try to amplify the impact of anything we do by finding the most unusual, remarkable, strange, unique, and ballsy angle to promote. We never do anything *normally*—that's what everyone else does, right?

Our secret sauce is our willingness to do things dif-

BALLS!

ferently—to push the envelope just enough to get noticed, but to still be taken seriously. We like to call it ordering "Off The Menu." Sometimes we are so far off the menu we're no longer in the restaurant. Ordering an item on the menu means that anyone else can do the same. That is far too normal and we wouldn't be noticed. To create a unique concoction that even the chef hasn't heard of is what we live for. In fact, if what we're doing doesn't feel at least a little bizarre, chances are it isn't going to attract the kind of attention we need to stand out in a crowd.

For example, when we throw a client appreciation party at a trade show, we do everything we can to make the party as memorable as possible for everyone who attends. Just the fact that we truly value our clients' time and appreciate that they are willing to spend it with us in and of itself makes our approach unique. Time really is money, and if they're spending both with us, we want them to get something they wouldn't get anywhere else.

Our "party off the menu" philosophy has two important benefits:

It creates a much stronger bond with our customers.

It makes life easier for our sales force because
NOBODY EVER FORGETS US!!!

Before we go any further and anyone accuses us of spending too lavishly on parties, let me set the record straight: We actually spend very little on parties. We don't use expensive event planners, and we often make our own invitations, and stuff and mail them from our office. Paper cuts, creative photocopy techniques, and assembly-line lunches are common around our office. We just make everything look, feel, and sound different even on a shoestring budget. We always make it fun. And we always, always track the return.

The second year I organized our appearance at a NADA trade show we had enough clients to throw a party. And that year the show was in New Orleans. We knew that everyone would be going to Bourbon Street to attend various parties. So we decided to throw a party not in some boring ballroom but literally in the lobby of the W Hotel. The hotel was one of the top host hotels and it was filled with tons of prospects. We could turn our "work hard, play hard" company mantra into the theme for our party—and turn the party into a living advertisement for our company. The hotel setting with hundreds of prospects roaming the halls would give us even more exposure than just the exhibit hall. In fact we would turn the hotel into our own exhibit hall.

The hotel was a deliberate choice as well. We knew that the kind of prospects who could afford to stay at one of the nicest, most innovative, and most expensive hotels

BALLS!

in the city were the kind of prospects we wanted to turn into clients. One face painter, four tattoo girls, and hundreds of blue ball martinis later, the party was legendary and actually got written up in the local society pages—in *New Orleans*!

The next year we took on San Francisco. Again we wanted to be different, so we timed our James Bond themed party with the release of the newest Bond film. Bond was everywhere through the city—seemingly promoting our party. Instead of taking over a hotel lobby, we decided to get more creative and take over an entire floor. We transformed the fourth floor of the W Hotel into an outlandish set from a myriad of Bond films. The pool became *For Your Eyes Only*, complete with Bond girls in bikinis. The outdoor terrace was *From Russia With Love*. Our fur-lined model lounged lavishly next to the vodka martini ice slide. You could find our head-to-toe *Goldfinger* girl next to the suite that was transformed into a casino. And Bond movies galore played on the TVs in all of the bedrooms we literally took over. We expected 500 clients and 1,500 showed up. Needless to say, the lines wrapped around the outside of the hotel and the multiple visits by the fire department created quite a buzz.

I guess projecting our logo on the fire station's wall gave us away, but I didn't hear any of the firefighters complain; in fact, I think they enjoyed the party more than anyone.

Last year we decided to have fun with the reputation we were getting for throwing standing-room-only parties with long waiting lines. We rented Studio 54 at the MGM Grand, and while the crowd of eager partygoers stood in line outside Studio 54, we transformed the line into a "blue carpet" award ceremony walk of fame. We hired a Joan Rivers impersonator to draw people out of the line and interview them. Our staff all dressed up as movie stars, and some even did impersonations. We hired striking models in skintight vinyl suits and stylish sunglasses to roam up and down the line. And we had "paparazzi" (our amazing attorney Bill Carleton assumed the role of Helmut Lang) pestering our clients to pose for their flashing cameras. We even printed up special "backstage pass" party passes and handed them to clients who stopped by our dramatic two-story booth at the trade show.

Once inside, there were enough pyrotechnics and soaring, scantily clad acrobatic dancers to satisfy anyone's need for a thrill fix. And to cap it off, we wangled comedian Howie Mandel to act as master of ceremonies. His blend of humor, intelligence and sheer off-the-wall wackiness fit perfectly with the scene we had created.

We also encouraged our guests to dress up in outlandish celebrity costumes and have their pictures taken with Las Vegas-style dancers. That way our guests helped us create the theme and atmosphere without costing us a dime. Then we created souvenir magazine covers for them to bring home—complete with photos documenting their wild night at Studio 54—giving us free advertising in their stores when they would show-case their souvenirs!

Afterward, people asked me how much money we had spent on the party. Some guessed that we'd spent upwards of $500,000 to pull it off. I just smiled—because we didn't spend anywhere near that amount. In fact, the deals we signed during and immediately following the convention more than justified our costs.

Follow, Follow, Follow the ROI Road

When I first interviewed Shellie Pierce for the job of event manager at Who's Calling, she didn't believe me when I told her that when we attend a trade show, we not only expect to see a return on investment (ROI) of between 300 to 400 percent but we pretty much demand it.

"I was very skeptical," recalls Shellie. "I'd worked on many trade shows and I'd never heard anything more than anecdotal evidence about actual sales. Most companies count leads and then hope they translate into sales, but often they never know. I'd certainly never met anyone who expected a 400 percent ROI from a trade show."

Now, after working with us for more than a year, Shellie is a true believer. "When Who's Calling decides to attend a trade show—or any event—we go in with guns blazing. Everyone is prepared, everyone is jazzed, everyone understands that the objective is making sales."

She's right. You can't miss us at a trade show. And you also can't miss our objective. Each person on the show floor is dressed exactly alike, usually in brightly colored Who's Calling trendsetting shirts, and we all know the sales goal for the day even if we aren't technically in sales. At a show we are all in sales. We arrive together, like a marching band—on a mission. We achieve our target ROI, or we simply won't do the event again. And when we make our number, we all cheer and pass out hundred dollar bonuses and play our theme songs—really loud!

Oh yes, our infamous theme songs—did I mention them yet? At our company you have to earn your theme song—usually for doing something unusual—and then once you have one, you have to embrace it. This tradition started with our sales team. They have always been a high-energy group. Adding music to the equation has only given them more ways to be innovative.

For example, we often play music in our booth at trade shows, and it's usually a rotation of theme songs. When your theme song plays, you have to dance or slide down our firefighters' pole—even if you're pitching a prospect. Let me tell you, the "dancing pitch" is one helluva way to get a potential client's attention, and of course we know it works since we track ROI on everything we do!

On top of our unusual high-energy antics, we always have a theme. One year it was Innovation and Talent, or IT for short. We created flashing IT buttons and made up an IT chant: *Got IT? Want IT? Get IT!* We even dressed any staff member who wasn't selling in either an "I" costume or a "T" costume and then made sure they walked the show floor—a lot—to hand out blue balls and even visit other booths at the show! We followed up by giving  Who's Calling Innovation and Talent (IT) Awards to five clients, reinforcing our commitment to supporting best practices in business.

Baby Your Leads . . . and Your Sales Team

Early on, I realized that my experience at Who's Calling would be unique. Every day brought some new and seemingly impossible challenge. Like the time when a salesperson's proposal-filled luggage was lost on the way to an important presentation across the country. We had two hours to re-create a detailed proposal for a major client before the 4:00 P.M. overnight delivery cutoff. We made it happen, stitching together content from his memory, our brochures, our Web site, old presentations, you name it. We were still assembling the proposal package when the delivery van drove up. Half the marketing team stayed behind to finish the proposal while the rest of us rushed out to flirt with the van driver and prevent him from leaving before we could hand him the package. Wow, talk about going the last mile for a deal! And it didn't end there. Then we had to spend an hour on the phone, briefing the sales manager on what we were sending to the client—and reassuring him that it would go off without a hitch.

As a marketing organization, we've always tried to act bigger and do more with less. We also do whatever it takes to help our sales team, foster the leads along the pipeline, and get the greatest return. That's our style, and it works. The alternative strategy would be to beg John or Stuart for more money—and that's not a strategy, that's a cop-out.

We've found that being aggressive, being loud, being different, and being a little wild make our marketing dollars go much farther than if we played the game like traditional buttoned-down business executives. Maybe that style of marketing worked in the Old Economy—but it sure doesn't work in the New Economy.

BALLS!

We've also found that we need to work closely with our sales team. At trade shows we make sure all our sales team needs to do is show up and look nice. We send them a detailed itinerary and custom clothing for each event. We ship breath mints and tape and pens and contracts to the show for them. We schedule group meals and events. We all work hard at the show and we all play hard when it's done.

Another way we take care of our sales team is to take better care of our leads. A few years ago we started to take the inbound leads into the marketing department rather than have them go directly to sales. By having our marketing staff answer the inbound calls, we not only created a real connection between their hard work and the prospects, but we also found out that we could make a great first impression on our prospects—all the while nurturing the leads a bit further down the pipeline, which helps our sales team spend more time on qualified prospects.

In-Your-Face Marketing

Sometimes you need to take the fight directly to a competitor's doorstep—and even a few steps further! Our friends at salesforce.com, a San Francisco–based technology firm traded on the New York Stock Exchange under the ticker symbol CRM, are also famous for their in-your-face approach to marketing. One of their favorite ploys is

77

 invading a competitor's user group conference and offering free coffee poured into mugs emblazoned with salesforce.com's unique "No Software" logo.

Another time they hired actors to picket a competitor's conference. Carrying signs that read "Don't Buy Software," the picketers marched around the entrance to the event while actors posing as journalists interviewed the picketers and conference visitors!

For a competitor's conference in Europe, salesforce .com hired taxi drivers to whisk visitors to the event in cabs decorated with the salesforce.com corporate logo.

"We use a tongue-in-cheek approach," says Parker Harris, one of the company's co-founders. "We try to keep the message humorous. It's a low-cost way to grab attention and to let people know that we're really different."

For a launch party, they rented a vintage San Francisco movie theater. On the lower level, actors sat in cells to symbolize the hellish aspects of enterprise software implementations. On the middle level, a band played a specially written "End of Software" theme song. At the balcony level, a woman played "heavenly" music on a harpsichord while guests sipped champagne and enjoyed dessert.

BALLS!

"Whenever we throw a party, we try to get the broadest range of people together," says Parker. "And the best part is that we don't try to sell them anything. We offer them a memorable, thought-provoking experience that they'll talk about long after the event is over."

Viral Transmission

Despite its worldwide success, salesforce.com remains true to its start-up nature. The company still prefers to spend its marketing dollars on off-the-wall promotions instead of on traditional advertising. There's method to this seeming madness.

"We thrive on word of mouth," explains Parker, who serves as the firm's senior vice president of research and development. "We want people to talk about us and to share their experiences with other people. That's the way we spread our message. Viral marketing has done more for us than any other kind of marketing."

I can testify to that. We use salesforce.com services at Who's Calling. We found out about the company from one of our clients, who raved about the quality and affordable price. Whether you call it word-of-mouth marketing or viral marketing, this kind of reverse marketing strategy—where the customers do most of the work—really works for companies with great products and reasonable pricing structures.

Everything You Need to Know in 30 Minutes

I don't know about you but lately I seem to "enjoy" most of my meals while on the go—grabbing an energy bar running between meetings, guzzling water from a plastic bottle, and, more often than I care to admit, having a liquid breakfast while sitting in my car, stuck in traffic.

The next time you're in your car sipping coffee from a stylish thermal mug, odds are the mug was designed and produced by Seattle-based Pacific Market International (PMI). More than 50 percent of PMI's revenues come from developing products for some of the world's largest consumer brands and retailers, including Starbucks, Target, Nike, Wal-Mart, and Tupperware.

PMI was founded in 1983 by Rob Harris, whom we'll meet up with again later on in the book. PMI's revenues have jumped impressively in the past few years, due in large part to Rob's unique understanding of Asian manufacturing processes. Twenty-three of PMI's 116 employees work in the firm's Shanghai office, giving them a secure toehold in this fast-growing market.

PMI is a small-size company with giant-size clients. Sometimes that size mismatch can pose a challenge. Big clients appreciate PMI's ability to produce innovative designs quickly and efficiently. But big clients often expect all

BALLS!

their vendors to act like big companies—even if they're not. That might seem unfair, but it's one of the harsh realities of doing business in today's global economy.

"It's important to project the proper image," explains Tami Fujii, PMI's vice president of marketing. "We've developed low-cost tactics that magnify the image we project to the world. We've become experts at developing highly dynamic, ultrapolished presentations and marketing collateral to communicate our strengths and capabilities."

PMI's promotional tactics are sophisticated, brave, and most definitely loud. Here's one I really love: A few years ago PMI came up with the idea to create a presentation called the *PMI Trend Perspective*. It's the result of an entire year's worth of research, writing, editing, and preparation, all done in-house by Tami's team. Their interactive 30-minute presentation covers the top consumer trends that impact buying decisions. Only PMI clients get to see the presentation, a concentrated dose of useful information about lifestyle product trends that they can then translate into product design and purchase decisions for their retail outlets.

"We try to cover every observable lifestyle trend, plus all the important social and economic macro trends. We collect, we sift, and we study ideas, articles, books, magazines, market research, and case studies from hundreds of industries and thousands of experts. Then we summarize this vast pool of information into one concise presentation." Whew, sounds like a lot of work!

"The first year it was," Tami admits. "Our office was filled with clippings, stats, photos, research books—you name it. But after we pulled it all together, we found that we had a tool that not only helped our clients but that also helped them see us as a partner, not just another product company."

The *PMI Trend Perspective* is designed to get the creative juices flowing. It reinforces PMI's reputation as a visionary organization that truly knows the market.

"We translate all the information into seven specific trends, offering clear, specific ideas that are easy to understand and highly actionable," explains Tami. "In 30 minutes our clients find out what's 'top of mind' for consumers in the coming year. And now each year we just update the original presentation when we see changes in specific trends or when new ones emerge."

PMI positions the presentation as a value-added service, offered to clients at no additional cost. Frankly, I think the *PMI Trend Perspective* is a brilliant idea. It allows PMI to stand out from its competitors and be loud—about its knowledge of consumers and industry trends. I plan to follow PMI's example—and you should, too!

BALLS!

Snag the Ideas!

Challenge conventional thinking and look for innovative ways to stand out from the crowd. For example, at trade shows, make a conscious effort to perceive the other vendors as opportunities, not as threats. With a little bit of creativity, you can turn a competitor into an asset or even jack a competitor's event. Here are some ways to accomplish this feat:

❶ *Everything is a reflection on you—even stuff you give away.*

Put your logo on only attractive, unique giveaway items— not chintzy ones—and make sure you give plenty of them to other vendors at trade shows. We're always amazed at how often we see other vendors bouncing our blinking blue balls—even while they're supposed to be marketing their own products. By making even your giveaway items unique and interesting you will get more people to keep them, and if they're of a high perceived value the recipients will subconsciously perceive your company in the same way.

❷ *Brand everything that isn't nailed down.*

Slap your logo on every moving object with a blank surface. Salesforce.com branded the taxicabs at a competitor's user conference, and we've rented limos for the day and placed a magnetized version of our logo on them.

83

Have the drivers travel between convention hotels to pick up clients. We've also often called up associations or trade show organizers and offered to donate items such as branded cocktail napkins or mugs. Can't afford the Goodyear blimp? You'd be surprised how inexpensive it is to have a small airplane tow a banner or simply rent a limo and place magnetic logos on it. (Make sure the plane flies over or the limo drives by while attendees are entering or leaving—there's no point in doing it while they're all inside eating lunch!) When you attend a trade show or event, brand your staff—at all times. Make sure everyone can see them a mile away. Dress them up in matching outfits, colorful costumes, and funny hats emblazoned with your logo. Wear flashing badges, glowing bracelets, or even just matching baseball caps—anything that will set you apart. Everyone will remember your team spirit and good humor. And you'll be amazed by how many resumes your human resources (HR) department will receive in the following weeks from people who attended the event and work for your competitors.

❸ *Take your theme to the extreme.*
Always look for unique ways to either hijack someone else's theme and take it to a new level or bring your own theme literally to the most unexpected places. We once attended a convention where the show's theme was "Dream Big! Make Your Wishes Come True." We didn't have a big budget, so to match the theme and take it to the extreme we bought inexpensive but large fairy wings,

BALLS!

blue wigs, plastic tiaras, and magic wands. During nonexhibit hours, our sales reps dressed up as fairy godmothers and "magically" appeared before prospects during lunches or evening receptions, bestowing small presents such as gift certificates for the hotel spa or Starbucks and explaining how Who's Calling would make their dreams come true. We were the talk of the show— and it cost us next to nothing!

❹ *Sometimes the best way to be loud is to be consistent.*
Lane Company, based in Atlanta, is a full-service multifamily real estate business. To maintain its strong position in the apartment and condominium markets, Lane has carefully positioned itself as the real estate company with a heart. Lane's branding campaign always projects a consistent message of inclusion—not as a result of fair housing compliance, but as a result of understanding that its business is about people. In word and deed, Lane demonstrates its devotion to serving all segments of the market. Lane's strong branding has illustrated a clear and unambiguous commitment to taking care of people and that is a "loud" distinguishing factor, giving Lane a competitive edge in a highly fragmented and intensely competitive market. Being consistent to your core message, or even having a message when others don't, will get you noticed and can help you win the race against your competitors.

Rule 4 — L is for Lovable

Rule 4 — L is for Lovable

When you love your employees, they not only love working for you, but they also pass that love along to your customers. They will lavish your customers with impeccable service. They will be passionate about your company and turn customers into raving fans. Talk about serious ROI: improved customer loyalty, lower marketing costs, and higher margins. In business, love *does* make the world go 'round. You can have good products and a great plan, but without taking care of people, you'll never reach the fourth "p"—profit. Simply put, make your company lovable.

("Morale is the greatest single factor in successful war."

~ Dwight D. Eisenhower)

Culture Counts

I admit it: This is my favorite part of *Balls!* No, not because you're still reading and I was told by my editorial director that on average, most people stop reading after the first three chapters (by the way, I'm out to prove him wrong). I love this part of the book because I get to write about our people and how lovable they really are. We have simply the coolest people on our team. And my friend Amy Ziegenbein, or "Amy Z," as we affectionately call her, takes care of us all.

Amy Z is the head of HR at Who's Calling. She's part-time therapist, part-time coach, and part-time engineer with a steady hand, who keeps the train on the tracks even as we speed headlong into unexplored and exciting new territory.

With nearly 300 employees, payroll represents a significant chunk of our spending. As we saw in the chapter entitled "A is for Authentic," small companies should strive for maximum productivity and efficiency to ensure healthy cash flow and avoid unnecessary debt. From an HR perspective, this means each person needs to contribute in a big way!

It has been said that first-rate leaders hire first-rate teammates, and second-rate managers hire third-rate employees. Every small or midsize company operating in a highly competitive market today needs to fine-tune a human capital strategy that includes hiring, training, nurturing, rewarding, and retaining a critical mass of the most

BALLS!

talented, energetic, action-oriented, entrepreneurial over-
achievers it can find.

And that's just the minimum.

Jack Welch, Move Over

There's no question that Jack Welch revolutionized the
corporate universe by flattening General Electric's notoriously cumbersome table of organization. But those were
the bad old days, when lumbering corporate leviathans
ruled the world economy. There are still plenty of them
out there, but they don't have the same monstrous clout
they used to—some elephants even dance!

Those of us fortunate enough to work at a growing,
fast-paced company know that complex reporting structures and intricate organization charts with lots of dotted
lines are worse than useless. Show me an org chart that
ever added value to a service or product.

Amy Z and her team help us create and maintain the
invisible infrastructure that supports and nourishes the
unique culture of Who's Calling. Without its special, lovable culture, Who's Calling would be just another strug-
gling company.

"We experienced our first major growth spurt a couple of years ago," recalls Amy. "As we began expanding,

we realized that we needed a clearly defined, ongoing strategy that would preserve and reinforce the qualities and capabilities of our founding team."

Building Success from Employee One

We were lucky to have had the foresight to plan for our growth, and the sheer will and focus to find ways to foster the kind of constructive culture we needed during periods of rapid growth. In just four short years I've personally witnessed us grow from 13 employees to nearly 300. It hasn't been easy, but by hiring right (not just quickly) and focusing on ways to foster our culture, we've been able to beat the odds and build a team of incredibly dedicated and passionate people.

In our second year of existence, Amy Z launched an in-house research project to identify and objectively measure the qualities of an ideal Who's Calling employee. "We took a group of our best employees and questioned them carefully to find out what made them stars. We identified eight qualities shared by these star employees. Then we developed a strategy to promote and reward these eight qualities across all of our activities as a company."

The strategy is proactive, employee-friendly, and rooted firmly in reality. It was embraced more rapidly and more completely than any similar strategy or program I've seen at other companies. I credit this to its

BALLS!

homegrown origins. If it had been thrust upon us by executive order—an unlikely scenario here, but not uncommon elsewhere—it probably would have faded into a dim memory by now.

Thanks to Amy Z, her department, and our management team, the eight qualities identified in a small group of early star employees are now woven into the fabric of our corporate culture. We've evolved those eight competencies over time and have regularly met with different employees to get their input on what these values mean to them and how they would demonstrate them in their jobs and departments. The eight employee core values are: innovation, client focus, integrity, enthusiasm, high performance, strong communication skills, team orientation, and accountability.

"Our core values are part of everything we do," says Amy. "They help us maintain that entrepreneurial culture of innovation, commitment, and agility that we need to succeed in our market."

When Amy's team interviews a job candidate, they look and listen carefully to make sure the candidate resonates with these values. "They are built right into our recruitment processes," says Amy. "We actively look for people who already have those qualities, because we know from experience they're going to succeed and that they're going to enjoy working here."

The core values are introduced formally to new hires during training sessions, which are run by seasoned Who's Calling employee volunteers. "All of our new hires are trained by at least two veteran employees who volunteer their time and share their knowledge. It's a great way of passing along our traditions and our values at a critical point in the new employee's life."

Our programs have evolved over time, as they should in a growing company. Our strategy for maintaining a consistent corporate culture includes several component programs, spanning a range of activities from recruiting to employee reviews to an innovative training curriculum called the Who's Calling Catalyst certification program.

Since personal and professional development are both important to us, we've partnered with the Pacific Institute to establish this unique program for accomplishing our goals of high individual and organizational achievement.

Starting with our executive management team, we made the commitment to involve the entire organization. In order to become a Who's Calling Catalyst, employees must graduate from courses taught by in-house, certified employee facilitators.

BALLS!

Have you heard that the greatest fear for the majority of people is public speaking? Death is second. Yet nearly 40 managers volunteered to become certified facilitators for our Catalyst training sessions. This reinforces our management's commitment to lead by example and to share their own experiences with a diverse group of participants from all parts of the company.

Today we have a core group of 10 employees and managers from various departments who regularly facilitate the curriculum over four days. Facilitating to the employee base has become a coveted position that brings as much learning and satisfaction to the seasoned facilitators as it does to the employees who are experiencing the material for the first time.

The Catalyst program starts with personal growth, but it also covers training and certification on all of our products and services. Employees learn how to remove barriers and limitations to personal and organizational growth, and develop a new sense of possibility. Each in-house session generates great discussions, bonding, and learning. As cross-functional groups of about 20 employees go through the programs, they create a group name and set up e-mail aliases to communicate with each other on topics and ideas that came up in their sessions. The program has been successful in breaking down silos and stimulating creativity among all of our employees.

The Who's Calling Catalyst certification program touches all departments and all aspects of life at Who's Calling, from our vision and values to reward programs to sales training on our services. It even touches on our management philosophies. It is the way things are done at Who's Calling—in a positive and constructive manner that allows employees and the organization to reach their full potential. Once an employee gets certified, demonstrating a level of knowledge and competency in a specific area, he or she receives a wristband in a specific program color. The bands become a badge of honor and are displayed like Olympic rings.

We've also developed a program called PASTE, which stands for People All Sharing Time and Experience. "We  like to say it's the glue that holds us together," Amy says with a smile. "Employees volunteer to be paired with a different employee each month—their PASTE buddy. The goal is to learn about different departments, share experiences, offer advice, or even sit down together for a friendly lunch."

Nearly half of our employees volunteered for the PASTE program, which is a testament to our ability to develop and promote these types of low-cost, high-value initiatives. By pairing our employees together in an informal setting we have created an environment where peers

BALLS!

foster the culture and motivate each other to extremely high levels of performance.

Cheers for CHEER!

Another program I really like is CHEER, which stands for Courteous, Helpful, Enthusiastic Excellence Reward. CHEER is our spot reward program, designed to reinforce the eight employee core values and provide immediate, tangible recognition for folks throughout the organization who live up to the high standards we've set.

Here's how it works: When a Who's Calling employee wants to show appreciation for the effort of a colleague, the employee goes to the CHEER folder on our shared hard drive and downloads one of nine distinct CHEER cards. There's a different card to recognize each of the eight core values, plus a wild card.

After downloading the appropriate card, the employee attaches the card to an e-mail message and sends it, along with a brief description of the colleague's achievement, to the colleague, often to their manager, and to HR.

Once an employee collects eight different core value cards or seven plus the wild card, he or she can redeem them through HR to receive a $15 gift certificate. An employee who collects eight different core value cards from eight different colleagues can redeem the cards and receive a $50 gift certificate.

"We also send out monthly updates and remind everyone to count their CHEER cards to see if they qualify for a gift certificate. This past May, for example, 267 cards were sent. Tan Ong from our finance team redeemed his CHEER cards for a gift certificate, and Reshelle O'Bryant from client services was top recipient of the month, with 11 cards in just one month. One nice aspect of this program is that it practically runs itself and the employees have a fun way to reward each other," says Amy.

Well, after all this talk about the cards, you deserve a look at them:

The Lonnie Card represents *innovation* and thinking totally out of the box. Makes sense, right?

The Eye on the Ball Card represents *client focus*, as in "we always keep our eye on the ball—our valued clients both internal and external." They are the reason for everything we do.

BALLS!

The Outreach Card represents *integrity.* We're dedicated to helping both our community and nationwide organizations. In addition to supporting Toys for Tots, Habitat for Humanity, and many other great causes, we support the Seattle Children's Hospital in an innovative way—by sponsoring a 100 percent charitable Team Seattle racing guild that raises per-lap donations for the 24-Hour Rolex Race in Daytona.

The IT Mascot represents *enthusiasm.* We often have our most enthusiastic employees dress up in a seven-foot-tall foam costume to celebrate IT—Innovation and Talent.

The Magic Carpet Card represents *high performance.* Speed and enjoying the ride are what it's all about. Also, our original all-company theme song was "Magic Carpet Ride," so it's also a nod to where we started and the actions our first employees took to get us on this ride.

The NOC Card represents *strong communication skills.* Our Network Operations Center (NOC) is the technological heart of Who's Calling and the industry's most advanced telecommunications center.

The Fish Tank Card represents *team orientation*. Lonnie and Dan love fish and we have some spectacular fish tanks around the office. Ever notice how fish swim together so gracefully and effortlessly?

The Imagine-21 Catalyst Card represents *accountability*. Our services show return on investments, and all of us are accountable, too. Our Catalyst training and certification for our people and services are examples of how we make this part of our culture.

The Manny Card is our *wild card*. Manny is a mannequin that we bring to trade shows and events. He's very loose and wild—you never know what to expect from this guy!

What Goes Around Comes Around

In addition to innovative programs such as PASTE and CHEER, we also create a full schedule of employee events and outings, all geared to reinforce our company values and bring us closer together. We have an annual rafting trip, a family Halloween party, Employee Appreciation Day, and employee anniversary recognition days. At least once a quarter we throw a surprise party or an ice cream sundae social.

We also don't skimp on employee awards. We give out a Brass Monkey Award (monthly award to one employee who did "whatever it takes"), an Innovator Award (quarterly award recognizing out-of-the-box thinking), a ROCSS award (award for Really Outrageous Client Services Superstar), a MAMA award (Most Amazing Marketing Achievement), a FAST award (Finance All-Star Team), a SPAM award (Superior Performance Achievement Medal for our operations team), an Outstanding HR Contributions Award (OHRCA—a "whale" of an award), a TPS award (Total Performance Award for Development—or maybe TPS reports, a tongue-in-cheek reference to the movie *Office Space!*), and many more. We also look for informal ways to encourage everyone to give his or her creativity free rein. For example, the employees got to name our conference rooms. Visitors find themselves attending meetings in the Blue Ballroom or The Tank (aptly named for its impressive fish tank, one of six in our corporate office), which in turn reinforces our focus on teamwork.

Although we love to party, not every perk requires a crazy celebration. We have a quiet room for anyone who just needs some time alone. Our Thursday chair massage is very popular, for obvious reasons. Every Friday is Free Bagel Friday. Every lunch hour our development team can be found playing XBox in the lunchroom. Every day is Free

Soda and Snapple Day, and there's always a fresh supply of M&Ms at Barb Edquist's desk in the friendly finance department in case anyone gets the craving for candy.

Speaking of our finance team, I bet it has the standing world record for winning our annual "dress up your department" Halloween theme and costume contest *every* year so far and counting. We even encourage department theme songs; and no, our finance team didn't get "Money" but instead "All Star" by Smashmouth because they really are an all-star team!

As I mentioned at the beginning of this chapter, the love we spend on our employees is never wasted. It almost always comes back to us with a dividend. Our clients sense the love and it gives them a good feeling. I'm proud to say that we're smart enough to leverage those good feelings into higher levels of client satisfaction. Wally Rex purposely named our customer service department our client satisfaction team, because they are and will always be totally committed not only to satisfying our clients, but also to exceeding their expectations and building higher rates of retention and loyalty.

Wally is now affectionately known as the Czar of Client Relations and he is free to spread the love nationwide. He travels the country to motivate our field sales force and personally meet many of our clients to ensure that they are

BALLS!

not just satisfied, but getting extreme return on their investment. And when he's traveling, he's sure to be caught playing the client satisfaction team theme song, "Ain't No Mountain High Enough" by the Groovetown Gang.

It's nothing new to focus on customer loyalty and to allocate budgets to more effectively grow relationships with existing customers, rather than just focusing on acquiring new customers. Loyal customers are not just a small company's valuable asset, but *every* company's greatest asset—aside from its people, of course.

Loyal customers—customers who love you and want to stay with you—represent more than a loose collection of individual business relationships. Loyal customers are an extended fam-ily, with all the interwoven, interdependent relationships of a flesh-and-blood family. At Who's Calling, loyal customers end up wearing our flamboyant hats at trade shows, they bounce our balls to prospects, and they jump in during a sales pitch to close a deal for us. Sometimes they even earn a theme song!

The idea of treating your customers as little more than revenue streams is not only cold, weird, and creepy—it's bad business. And yet so many companies, despite their claims to the contrary, are still locked into an accountant's eye view of the universe. Stuart DePina and his team don't have this view. In fact, our finance department actively looks for ways to interact with clients in positive ways before they have to make a credit or collections call. Through telephone calls and written communications, they begin building relationships with the finance departments of our clients as soon as the ink on the contract dries.

"Our first contact with our clients is not along the lines of 'You haven't paid your bill on time,' " says Diane Hager, our finance director. "We try to build a relationship with our peers in the finance departments of our clients, the same way our client satisfaction team works with our clients' service reps, or the same way our sales managers work with our clients' managers on how to use our products and services."

Diane sees herself as a key part of the client relationship cycle, not just part of the revenue process. It's her kind of approach that makes our clients feel loved.

A Company of Friends

You can talk all you want about analyzing customers from the perspective of their net present value, their lifetime value, or their maximum potential value, but the simple truth is that your customers are people and all people want to be loved. Love them and they'll stay with you forever.

The best way to begin the process of loving your customers is by loving your employees. End of sermon!

Hold on. One more story to share before we leave the subject. We recently surveyed 165 employees and discovered that 67 percent of our employees were referred to Who's Calling by a friend or family member before they began working here, 59 percent have a friend or family member who currently works or worked at Who's Calling, 68 percent have referred a friend or family member for a job here, and 95 percent say they would recommend a family member or friend for a job here. Of the respondents to the survey, half took the time to share a detailed anecdote of how they became a Who's Calling employee. In fact, they shared enough interesting anecdotes to fill another whole book.

It was amazing to see how many of our colleagues were recruited by friends or relatives who were already happily employed here. That's a pretty strong endorsement for maintaining a humane and caring corporate culture. Remember the archaic days of companies mandating that you couldn't have family members work together?! Rules don't make a better culture; great people do. Great people are often related to great people, plain and simple. Our first salesperson was Lonnie's sister, Karen Jansen (and she's still one of our most enthusiastic account executives), so I guess it all started there. And I'm actually married to one of our vice presidents, but you'll hear from him a little later.

Many of the companies we work with also share our

values. One that comes to mind is salesforce.com, a firm that honors the business value of being loving and lovable.

Sharing the Love

In the previous chapter, we visited briefly with sales-force.com, the innovative provider of on-demand customer relationship management (CRM) services. If you haven't heard of Marc Benioff, the company's chairman and CEO, please allow me to introduce him to you.

Marc, along with Parker Harris, Dave Moellenhoff, and Frank Dominguez, founded salesforce.com in the spring of 1999. Their idea was to create Web-based software that would replace traditional enterprise software technology. Marc and his colleagues are the unofficial heralds of a movement they call "The End of Software." Their position is that Web-based applications can deliver immediate benefits at reduced risks and lower costs than enterprise applications.

By now, this doesn't seem like such a far-out notion, but back in 1999 it was practically heresy. Marc and his friends didn't care, though. They sensed the world was ready for change.

Before innovative companies such as salesforce.com and Who's Calling made it possible for small firms to develop their own CRM strategies and track return on their in-

BALLS!

vestments, only large corporations could afford the software required to implement a CRM program. If you weren't among the Fortune 1000, you could read all you wanted to about CRM, but you couldn't practice CRM at your own company, because the up-front costs of the technology were too steep—until guys like Marc Benioff and Lonnie Benson came along and showed the world that anyone who understood the value of a loyal customer base could benefit from CRM without pawning the family heirlooms.

Like our own Lonnie, Marc is truly unique. Early in his career, Marc decided that information technology could be harnessed to generate positive social change. He proved that you can share the love with your employees and with your clients—and then you can go several steps beyond that and share your love with the whole world. In July 2000, with Colin Powell looking on, Marc launched the salesforce.com/foundation, a global philanthropic organization whose goal is bridging the digital divide. Marc jump-started the foundation with $2.5 million of his own cash.

Marc also pioneered the "1 percent solution" for companies that want to make tangible contributions to society. Under the 1 percent solution, a company contributes 1 percent of profits, 1 percent of equity, and 1 percent of employee hours to the communities it serves.

Marc co-authored *Compassionate Capitalism* (Career

Press, 2004), a best practices guide for corporate philanthropy. The World Economic Forum named Marc as a "Global Leader of Tomorrow." *Computerworld* made him an Honors Laureate. The government of Israel gave him the Promise of Peace award for using technology to further peace in the Middle East. The nonprofit organization HEAVEN (Helping Educate, Activate, Volunteer, and Empower via the Net) gave him a Bridge Award for providing Internet access to the underserved in America's inner cities.

And yet this busy guy still finds the time to run a publicly traded company that manages customer information for 10,700 customers and 161,000 paying subscribers, including Automatic Data Processing (ADP), Advanced Micro Devices (AMD), SunGard, Corporate Express, Dow Jones, America Online (AOL), Avis/Budget Rent A Car (Cendant Rental Car Group), Polycom, SunTrust Banks, and Who's Calling.

A Whole Different Culture
Okay, most of us don't have access to millions of dollars to give back to the world. So I'd like you to meet another good friend, Jack Shimota of Walser Automotive Group in Hopkins, Minnesota. Hopkins is a growing suburb in the southwest corner of Minneapolis. Dozens of automobile dealerships there fight tooth and nail for their share of the local market.

Among the most successful are the dealerships owned

by the Walser Automotive Group. One of the factors contributing to Walser's overall success has been its long-standing commitment to keeping its customers and community happy. At Walser, customer satisfaction is a key element of the compensation plan.

The sales teams at Walser don't work on commission. Instead, their pay is based on measured levels of customer satisfaction. In other words, their customers have to love them—or they don't make money.

Jack Shimota, a group vice president, is based at Walser's Chrysler Jeep dealership. He's been at Walser for the past 27 years. He started as a salesman. He knows that customer loyalty and employee loyalty are two sides of the same coin.

"If your employees are happy and you take care of them, they'll take care of you," says Jack. "We try to develop a strong sense of loyalty between the sales staff and their customers. We want our customers to feel like they're a part of our family."

Like Amy Z, Jack has developed a fresh approach to the hiring process. "I look at new hires very differently today," he says. "In the past, when I found people with great customer skills but poor negotiating skills, there really wasn't a place for them. When I look back, it seems to me that some of those folks would have made great salespeople today. In the old days, the salespeople had to be ready for a certain amount of confrontation. But not everybody can handle confrontational situations, so we lost a lot of good people."

Isn't it amazing how times have changed? Do you remember going into an automobile showroom with your dad? Remember all the macho nonsense that would take place between the salesman and your dad as they haggled over features and prices? It all seems like a crazy waste of time and energy now.

"We changed to a one-price system about a year ago and it changed our whole philosophy toward sales. Now the salespeople get a flat dollar amount for every car sold, regardless of profit," explains Jack. "But if the salesperson's Customer Satisfaction Index (CSI) is 95 percent or better, there's a bump in pay. Salespersons with high CSIs will earn more money per deal than salespersons with low CSIs."

The result has been a major cultural change. The sales team's focus has shifted from making deals to growing long-term, profitable relationships with delighted customers. The sales team's role has become more strategic and less purely tactical. There's a two-week training program at corporate headquarters for new hires, followed by another two weeks of training at the dealership. There are daily training sessions at each dealership.

BALLS!

"In the old days we hired people and said, 'There's the showroom, now go out and sell.' Now we do training every day. We talk all the time, trying to figure out the best way to beat the competition. We're constantly looking for new ideas to try. That's how we stay ahead of the game."

It's about Relationships, Not Just Deals

Now the big question facing Jack and the other executives at Walser is how to leverage the company's size and reputation to create more opportunities for sales and profit.

"Here's a typical challenge: What's the best way to sell a car that's not a Chrysler to one of our loyal Chrysler customers? Let's say the Chrysler customer wants to buy a used Toyota for his college-age daughter. In the past, we might have sent him across town to our Toyota dealership. Now, we check the Walser intranet first and see if we have the car he's looking for at any of our other locations. If we find the car, we call the dealer and we bring the car here, to the Chrysler dealership. That might not seem like rocket science, but it's a smarter move than sending the customer out to wander all over town looking for a Toyota. What if he winds up buying the car from a dealer that's part of another group? Not only would we lose the individual sale, we might lose the entire relationship with the customer."

Can you imagine a car guy talking like that 20 years ago? As Jack says, "It's a whole different culture today."

Ask the Customer

As you might expect, Jack doesn't mind putting his customers on a pedestal. He figures they deserve it; not only do they generate income, they also generate actionable business intelligence. Walser surveys every customer who purchases a vehicle or brings a car in for service.

"If you ask the customer a question and you listen carefully to the answer, chances are good that you will learn something you need to know," Jack tells his staff. "Maybe it's something as simple as changing the brand of coffee you're serving."

Sometimes what you learn from your customers can save you from losing a competitive advantage. "A while ago we cut back on our evening service hours," recalls Jack. "At the time we made the decision, we didn't know that one of the major reasons people bought cars from us was because they really liked our evening hours. When we tracked all the calls we were missing through Who's Calling's service and we saw that our customer

 surveys revealed our mistake, we quickly extended our hours again. It turned out that our longer hours were a genuine competitive edge."

There is one quality that Jack shares with the car salesmen of the bygone past: his instinct for competition. The main dif-

BALLS!

ference is that Jack's competitive time frame spans decades. He views competition from a strategic, long-term perspective. "We're blessed to be in a market with lots of great competitors," he says. "So we keep our eyes and ears open. That's how we anticipate the needs of our customers. That's how we win."

Resisting the Easy Way Out

When the dot-com boom went bust in 2001, Kit Jeerapaet's instinct was to preserve the people around him. It's an admirable instinct and it's also ballsy, especially in a tough economy. Here's his story:

Kit is president of *duPont Registry* magazine, a luxury item publication based in St. Petersburg, Florida. With a paid circulation of more than 100,000 and a newsstand price of $6.95, it's one of the most profitable automobile magazines in history; it doesn't include one line of editorial copy. The typical reader has an annual household income of $200,000 and $2 million in assets.

"We reach the wealthiest demographic and we're consistently among the top three car magazines in newsstand revenue," says Kit. "We've been doing this for nearly 20 years, but we're always looking for new angles."

In 1999, one of those "new angles" arose. Kit remembers it well. "We are a marketplace for high-end luxury items. At the height of the dot-com era, we decided to leverage our reputation and create an online auction business. It would be like eBay, except you could buy Picasso paintings, Rolex watches, and other luxury items."

Venture capitalists absolutely loved the idea and promised carloads of cash to finance the new business. "We split the existing company and set up a dot-com to operate the auction site. We figured we'd run the site for a couple of years and then sell it to eBay."

Looking back on it, Kit says the plan was "crazy." But it was hard to resist the siren song of the venture capitalists. "We had millions and millions of second-round financing. We were ready to go public."

Then the stock market tanked, the dot-com boom fizzled, and Kit had to scrap his plans for an IPO. "After the market crashed, there was no way we could go public. We needed a new strategy—fast."

With the blessing of the company's owners, Kit dissolved the auction company and went back to the drawing board. "I realized that if we refocused on our original identity and we went back to our core business, we would recover whatever ground we'd lost."

Kit didn't want to fire the people he'd brought on

BALLS!

board to launch the auction site, but he needed a new business model that would be compatible with the core enterprise. And he needed it quickly.

Over the years, *duPont Registry*'s loyal readers had evolved into a global community of like-minded individuals. The duPont Registry brand had been extended to include magazines about luxury boats, celebrity cars, fine homes, and upscale urban lifestyles.

"We are a marketplace—plain and simple. Our magazines have no editorial, just ads. People read our magazines because they want to buy high-end cars, boats, or homes. Instead of trying to reinvent ourselves, we decided to build an online version of the marketplace we'd already created."

Kit had to first convince everyone that the online magazine was a good idea. Then he had to convince his boss not to outsource the project to a prominent Web development firm that was a tenant in the duPont Registry building with a staff of more than 100 developers. "We could have done a barter deal for no cash. But I knew that if we kept the project in-house, our people would put their hearts and souls into the new site." And he could keep his employees.

It took balls to start another online venture after one

had just failed. Kit was smart enough to foresee—and brave enough to acknowledge—that building his new business model would invariably involve mistakes. "I knew that only about 80 percent of my decisions would be accurate. I knew I would make mistakes, and I didn't want to be at the mercy of an outside Web developer who didn't understand our needs. Doing the project in-house gave us the flexibility and the accountability we needed to make sure everything worked the right way."

Kit's gamble paid off nicely. With most of his original staff intact, he created a new online business from scratch. Today, duPontREGISTRY.com augments and enhances the experience offered by the magazines. It adds a dimension of immediacy to the mix by enabling buyers to find sellers in the time it takes to point a cursor and click a mouse. It also appeals to buyers who do their research and shopping online. It's the world's leading online marketplace for Ferrari, Porsche, Mercedes-Benz, BMW, Lamborghini, Hummer, Aston Martin, Bentley, Rolls-Royce, and many other luxury cars.

If you visit the duPont Registry office building, you will see just how nicely the gamble paid off. Many of the employees can now afford to drive the exotic cars they all love and market so well. Some even drive their glamorous cars right into the office lobby!

116

Here's the moral of this tale: If Kit had caved in and taken the easy way out of his dilemma by firing his loyal staff, he wouldn't have the resources at hand to launch the business that has proven so wildly successful. That's my idea of a lovable guy!

Snag the Ideas!

A couple of months before *Finding Nemo* was released on DVD, Lonnie preordered dozens of copies. The morning they arrived, Lonnie put one on the desk of every Who's Calling employee with a child or who simply wanted one. On Halloween, Lonnie sends everyone home early—so they can go trick-or-treating with their kids. In today's world, a business can't succeed unless its people are passionate about their work. Ignite the passion by taking good care of your people. When they feel loved, they're more likely to go the extra mile to make sure the clients are happy. Here are some ideas for elevating the levels of love throughout your organization:

❶ *Try random acts of kindness with your employees. Sometimes the smallest things at the most unexpected times will produce the greatest return. For example, our management team unofficially likes to schedule at least one surprise social event each quarter. We've hosted Friday lunch barbeques on the office lawn. We've rented a local*

theater and taken employees to a movie premiere. We've even had the managers serve the staff at an old-fashioned ice cream sundae social. Team-building events make a difference, especially when they encourage interdepartmental bonding. And they don't have to cost a lot. Get creative with a team "photo hunt" tied into your company's vision and values. If one of your core values is open communication, a team might snap a photo of an open door to an executive office or a bulletin board filled with messages.

2 *Doing good can be good fun.*
If you're holding a charity drive, turn it into an event that spreads good feelings among your employees. We used to hold annual drives to collect food, clothing, and school supplies for needy families. Now we pair each fund-raising event with a company-wide employee event, usually hosted by a different department each time. Our development department holds the record for the most innovative school supplies drive—an authentic Mexican fiesta. In return for collecting supplies or donating cash, the staff got to enjoy Mexican food and kick back a little early on a Friday afternoon. We raised nearly $800 and gathered five large boxes of supplies—and everyone enjoyed playing hooky!

3 *Flexibility is key, especially when it involves taking care of customers.*
Teresa Bordenet, one of our original employees and now a senior manager on our client satisfaction team, urges

BALLS!

her staff to work unusual hours. "Often I encourage them to call or to visit clients in the early evening or on weekends. The clients are pleasantly surprised, which usually puts them in a better mood. We also get to spend more quality time with them because they're usually less busy at odd hours than they are during the day. And my folks like it because they get time off during the regular workweek in exchange for working odd hours!"

❹ *Mix it up between departments and levels.*
We all know that the more approachable your management team is the better. We also know that sometimes that kind of open communication and interaction simply doesn't happen all that often. Here's a great way to encourage interactions between employees and top executives. We have each member of our management team take turns to personally hand out the paycheck deposit statements to all employees twice a month, which creates opportunities for spontaneous interactions at all levels of the company. Some of our best ideas have arisen from chats between John and a client services rep or Wally and a software development technician. For remote employees we've invited different "executive guest speakers" to join department conference calls.

❺ *Very Important Practice—VIP service.*
Ted Loughead of Loughead Pontiac GMC Nissan gives all of his returning customers a special VIP toll-free number from Who's Calling to call for service. Not only does this

number let his staff know by an automatic alert message, a "whisper," that a returning customer is calling, it lets his customers know that he values them and makes an effort to treat them well. Try this and you'll see customer satisfaction increase. Every time returning customers call or visit your business, make certain they receive VIP treatment. Never put them on hold. Route their calls to your most experienced reps. If you miss a call from them because your office was closed, call them back regardless of whether they left a message. With today's technology, there's no excuse to not find ways to identify and treat all your loyal customers like VIPs.

6 *Love them like your mother.*
Jeff Schrier Ford in Omaha, Nebraska, totally empowers its staff to go the extra mile—literally! It has even given its customer care strategy a name: "Love Them like Your Mother." Recently, a customer was involved in an accident in New Jersey while on a family vacation. It was Friday night, but within two hours a trailer with a replacement minivan was on its way to the stranded family, saving their vacation. Everyone at Jeff Schrier Ford is taught to treat customers like family, even if it means initially sacrificing profit to provide additional service. What goes around will eventually come around back to you.

7 *Don't just use CRM as a catchphrase or tool.*
Just because you say you "have a CRM" doesn't mean you practice true customer relationship management. Don't as-

BALLS!

sume that everyone even knows what CRM stands for, or that they understand the customer relationship management processes or even what it means to build relationships. Cathy Ellico, the CRM/e-commerce manager at Jaguar Land Rover, works diligently with 170 Jaguar retailers and 160 Land Rover retailers to maximize the potential of their CRM investments—whatever they may be. "Sometimes people think that CRM is a technology. It's a process that's enabled by technology. CRM helps us meet the high expectations of our customers on a consistent basis because it puts detailed customer knowledge at the dealer's fingertips," says Cathy. "CRM enables you to maintain the 'Cheers' bar atmosphere—where everybody knows your name. For us, that's an important competitive advantage."

Rule ❺ — S is for Spunky

Rule ⑤ — S is for Spunky

What does it mean to be spunky? I think that spunky is a blend of bravado, cleverness, inspiration, and determination. Spunky is going where no one has gone before. Spunky is doing the unexpected; when everyone else jigs, you jag.

Spunky is following your own best instincts, following the feelings that make you what you are—even if you have to fight the tide or buck the status quo. I credit a large part of the continuing success of Who's Calling to our spunky approach to the market. We don't follow the old trails; we blaze new ones. Sometimes it's a rough hike to get where we need to go, but the extra effort almost always pays off.

Spunky companies stay close to their customers and know what they are thinking. Spunky companies are *never* caught off guard or surprised by sudden shifts in the market. Spunky companies have the confidence to move into uncharted territory and be wildly innovative. Leaping ahead of the competition involves taking risks, but that's what being spunky is all about—staying in front of the wave. Not waiting, but jumping right in and paddling as hard as you can!

("Only those who risk going too far can possibly find out how far one can go.")

~ T.S. Eliot

Innovate or Die

In addition to having a brave heart, Lonnie Benson has a spunky soul. In his current role as chief product architect, Lonnie leads our research and development team. The only rule they follow is: There are no rules! Sometimes I think they would rather die than not innovate. Modeled after legendary groups such as Lockheed's Skunkworks and Disney's Imagineers, Lonnie and his team are focused on the future. They even have a "Mind Map" to keep track of all their wild new ideas.

"I'm amazed at the things we've done so far, but it's nothing compared to what we are going to do," says Lonnie. "We're discovering new markets, and developing new products. We're looking at the world with fresh eyes and figuring out new ways to do things—that's what I really live for, aside from my incredible kids, of course. If you don't continually change and innovate, how can you survive?"

And if you've ever seen Lonnie with his kids, five-year-old Anna and seven-year-old L.J., you know where he gets his inspiration. They are brave and spunky—just like their dad. And like their dad, they're always doing something unexpected.

MARs to the Rescue

Speaking of kids, have I mentioned that three of John Stapleton's children (they're grown-up so I won't reveal their ages!) are sales executives at Who's Calling? Sean, Kate, and Meg Stapleton are three of our hardest-working and most dedicated sales execs. Maybe it's in their genes. Or maybe they picked up the knack from being around their father.

One thing is certain: Kate Stapleton's spunkiness helped us solve a problem that threatened to erase a chunk of our profits in 2003. It was a problem that is common to many young and ambitious companies: We were great at acquiring new customers, but not always focused on ensuring they received the full value of all features and services.

We had created a new market, but we were no longer the only players in it. We had the quality, the people, the brand, and the expertise, but there were competitors willing to cut corners and drop their prices to win a share of the market.

Our attrition rates began rising. We knew we were selling the best products and the best services in the market, but our competitors were turning our first-mover advantage against us by waging an aggressive price war.

We took action on a number of fronts. But Kate, our director of sales services, really helped us turn the tide. Here's how she did it: Kate knew that we kept precise records showing exactly how each client used our various services. Keeping detailed usage reports is a part of our standard service contract, but very few of our clients ever actually looked at these records.

Kate saw a terrific opportunity. She took the records, boiled them down to a manageable report of essential business metrics showing key monthly trends for each client. In essence, she created a new service that would bring additional value to our clients at no additional cost.

Kate's brainchild created a valid reason for each of our account executives to sit down and spend some quality time with his or her clients, on a regular basis, to discuss the report and focus on how we could help their business, not just deliver data.

These Monthly Account Reviews (MARs, for short) have quickly become one of our most effective home-grown tactics for building customer loyalty. Essentially, the MARs allow our sales team to resell Who's Calling

BALLS!

every month and bring our clients value they simply can't get anywhere else.

"It's not only a monthly reminder of how we're helping the client," says Ed Parkinson, one of our original and most experienced sales executives. "It actually shows exactly which parts of the client's sales process are delivering value and which need improvement, month by month."

MARs are handed to clients in face-to-face meetings, which guarantee opportunities for meaningful dialogues between our sales reps and our clients. "The MARs clearly show each client the return on his or her investment in Who's Calling, so there's no question about whether or not we're delivering genuine value. The MARs also highlight specific areas where more resources are required, or where spending can be reduced," says Ed. For a company that uses technology, having old-fashioned face-to-face interactions to bring even more valuable information to clients is a surprisingly unique concept.

The MARs have empowered our team to morph themselves into consultants, raising the perceived value of each sales visit and elevating the overall quality of the relationship. Instead of perceiving the sales rep as someone trying to sell something, the client sees the sales rep as an irreplaceable resource—someone who knows more about the client's business than the client and who is willing to share valuable, actionable knowledge every month.

"For our clients, the MARs are a highly useful management tool," says Ed. "For us, the MARs are a very effective tool for deepening our customer relationships. The deeper the relationship, the more likely it is to last. It has truly been an exciting ride to be a part of a sales team that has transitioned from just selling products to now showing the true value of our services."

The MARs really helped us push back the competition without resorting to price warfare that could have cost us dearly. We've had competitors literally try to *give* their products away just to gain market share. The MARs help us remind our clients that you get what you pay for. Most of our clients prefer to work with a partner who cares about them and who doesn't resort to holding fire sales to win business.

In a real way, our industry is similar to the modern retail automotive industry. Successful dealerships avoid price wars—they compete on the basis of service and value. We do, too.

It was impressive to see how quickly our sales team integrated the MARs into their routine. For the sales force, the MARs serve as constant reminders that we're bringing

BALLS!

real value to our clients. They help our sales reps remember all the good things we do, so they fall in love with the products and services they're selling, all over again. It's all in the MARs.

Reinventing the Sales Force

There's no question that the MARs are a great tool for establishing consultative relationships with our clients. But transforming a sales force from a selling organization into a consulting organization requires more than just one tool. It requires an enormous change in mind-set.

Being spunky requires nerve and imagination. It usually also requires a stiff backbone and a thick skin. My husband Dave Venneri is vice president of sales at Who's Calling (yes, I referred someone, too).

As I've suggested earlier, our sales force is rapidly evolving from a loose pack of sharp-eyed hunters into a tightly knit, well-managed team of experienced cultivators. As you might expect, the evolution hasn't been entirely free of pain.

"In the early years, it was sell, sell, sell," says Dave. "We didn't normally go back to see if the client was happy with the product. If we didn't hear from them, we assumed everything was fine. Today, our sales team focuses on building relationships with their clients and creating tighter bonds that will give us competitive advantages for years to come and really bring more value to the clients."

With the sales team focused on keeping clients satisfied, top management can concentrate on opening new markets for our products and services. "Our mission isn't selling technology. Our mission is helping organizations radically improve their sales process. That requires establishing a level of trust where the client is comfortable with us becoming an integral, embedded part of their sales effort," says Dave. "In a very real sense, we're asking them to outsource a major piece of their sales process to us."

Assembling a sales team that could execute on this vision required Dave to make some hard decisions. "We knew we would have to change the compensation plan to provide incentives for managing customers. Under the old plan, sales reps were paid a small base salary but received high monthly residuals for the life of each client they signed. Under the new plan, sales reps are paid a much higher base salary and receive a small percentage of the total monthly billing of their managed account base."

Basically, the old compensation plan rewarded people who were good at finding new accounts, and the new comp plan rewards people who are good at managing established accounts. Much like Jack Shimota and his team, our managers are now motivated and rewarded to take

BALLS!

care of our valued clients instead of being encouraged to simply hunt down their next sale. As you can imagine, there were some who did not greet the new plan warmly.

"We had some turnover, and it was a learning experience," recalls Dave. "But the world doesn't end when a comp plan changes. Life goes on and everyone adjusts to the new circumstances. The honest truth is that if we had kept the old plan, we probably would have lost clients and eventually driven ourselves right out of business. Instead we kept clients and employees—employees who recognized the importance of building client relationships. We now attract people who really understand how to bring incredible value and unsurpassed service to our clients."

Sounds good, but has it worked? Well, right before we reinvented the sales force, we were marginally profitable. After reinventing the sales force, we were able to significantly increase profits—all in less than a year. "John made it very clear to us that Who's Calling would change for the better, or die trying. For those of us who love the company, that's plenty of incentive!"

Bleed Blue

To pull off such a spunky shift in mind-set and direction also required a uniquely innovative communications plan. One of our strategies to ensure a steady stream of useful communication between the corporate headquarters in Seattle and our field sales offices across the nation has been to reinvent our own version of a nationwide concert tour. We called ours the Bleed Blue Tour. Basically, it is a nationwide road trip that happens twice a year. Here's how it works:

Every six months, we gather 50 of our 100 sales execs for two days of group training sessions in one regional location. They are from two different sales regions to ensure diversity and to encourage sharing of knowledge. Our corporate executives and subject matter experts also attend the Bleed Blue sessions, to teach and to learn.

"The goal of Bleed Blue is sharing best practices and extending the family atmosphere of corporate headquar-ters into the field," explains JoAnn Bercot, our sales operations manager, who acts much like a road manager for our Bleed Blue Tours. "It's not just about learning—we make sure it's fun, too!"

For example, everyone who attends or organizes the events has his or her own theme song, and whenever they make a presentation or receive an award, the theme song plays over the sound system. Holly Crace, our event manager, used to have the theme song "I Get

BALLS!

Knocked Down" by Chumbawumba, but she eventually earned "Tiny Dancer" by Elton John. JoAnn's song is "She Works Hard for the Money" by Donna Summer. My theme song is "Shake Your Groove Thing" by Peaches and Herb. Each song comes with a unique story behind it (bribes *sometimes* work if you want to find out the story behind a song), and there's nothing better than a publicly embarrassing moment to get you stuck with a song!

"We burn CDs with everyone's theme song and print up Bleed Blue Tour T-shirts with the date and location of the session," says JoAnn. "We also give away customized sun visors and prizes—anything we can think of to boost morale and create a spirit of togetherness."

In addition to getting everyone up to speed on the latest products and training our field team to use our various administrative tools, the Bleed Blue sessions serve another important role: They help us spot emerging talent. As each of the reps gives a presentation or shares a best practice, it's a chance for our corporate executives to observe the next generation of leaders—before they even know they're leaders!

"The Bleed Blue Tours are expensive, but the return is easy to measure because there's an increase in sales," says John Stapleton. "Sales increase because everyone is energized, psyched up, and so much more prepared for success. They've spent two days sharing war stories and trading tips, so they feel like they're ready for anything. It's like getting the family together from all parts of the country for a big reunion. You can't tell the new family members from the old because we all learn a lot from each other."

We also use the Bleed Blue Tours to rehearse sales techniques and practice customer relationship management skills. Bleed Blue gives us a chance to remind ourselves that our mission isn't selling technology; our mission is solving business problems for our clients, swiftly and cost-effectively. That's a lot different from the old "sell, sell, sell" mantra.

Catalysts of Change

As a part of our shift to become more consultative, we have also taken a look at all of our offerings. We are keenly focused on providing products and services that are not just marketed as sales catalysts but that are measurable. More recently, we are positioning our sales and customer support teams as catalysts, too.

Matt Stroh, our director of services marketing, explains why. "Before we launch a new service or product, we certify the service as a Sales Catalyst™. That means each product or service has been tested and proven effective in real-world situations, by real clients. The goal is to

BALLS!

remind the market that we provide practical solutions for actual business challenges."

Since our employees are now an essential and irreplaceable part of our service offerings, it made sense to certify them also. It's another way of letting the marketplace know that we're very serious about delivering the best possible sales experience.

As I mentioned in the previous chapter, we have a special team of trainers devoted to our Catalyst program, and Wally Rex spends much of his time in the field ensuring that certification standards are being achieved. Becoming certified as a Sales Catalyst is a point of pride at Who's Calling. It means you fully understand the company's mission and that you're fully qualified to meet the needs of our clients.

"The Catalyst certification ensures a high level of training, confidence, and enthusiasm," says Matt. "Those high levels of proficiency and passion translate into better, more profitable customer relationships."

A Ticket to China

Making a strategic and large-scale transition in your business model is no small task. A few chapters ago, I told you about Pacific Market International and its innovative *PMI Trend Perspective* presentation. Now I'd like to revisit

PMI and tell you the story of its spunky co-founder and current chief executive officer, Rob Harris. Despite incredible odds, Rob has succeeded in making large-scale changes in a huge market.

Rob grew up in Summit, New Jersey. Armed with a graduate degree in psychology from Syracuse University, he went to work as a psychotherapist at a large psychiatric hospital in northern New Jersey.

It didn't take him long to find out that he didn't want to spend the rest of his life as a psychotherapist. "My colleagues seemed less happy than their patients," he recalls. "I decided that I needed to do something totally different."

For Rob, "something totally different" was setting up an international trading company. "It was 1983 and everyone was talking about business opportunities in Asia. I went around to all the local companies and asked them for lists of products they currently bought in the United States. I told them I was going to China and that I would find them the same products for 20 percent less. Pretty soon I had a pocket full of purchase orders. I bought an airplane ticket to Hong Kong. When I arrived, I quickly discovered that it's great to be a buyer in a part of the world where everyone is trying to sell something."

But Asia wasn't—and still isn't—a paradise for wandering American capitalists. Rob soon realized that the

BALLS!

real challenge in Asia isn't finding companies to fill purchase orders. The real challenge is finding the *right* companies in Asia, companies with whom American firms can partner and grow. Meeting that challenge—the challenge of forming long-term business relationships with companies in Asia—became Rob's career.

Over time, PMI has evolved from a trading company into a product development and marketing company that now partners with manufacturers in Asia. Despite its continual evolution, PMI still sees relationship management as a critical core competency.

"What I've learned from my years of doing business in Asia is that the relationship is everything," says Rob. "If you're looking to partner with a factory in China, you've got to be ready to go out into the countryside and drive maybe five or six hours to a village in the middle of nowhere. You'll sit and talk with the factory owner for hours. You'll talk about his family, you'll talk about the weather, you'll talk about sports—and that's just to get a price quote! If you *really* want to do business, you'll have to hang out at the factory for days, observing, chatting, eating, asking questions, answering questions, and becoming part of the fabric of life there."

The purpose of an extended visit isn't purely to form social bonds. "You need to know what's going on or your partnership will fail," says Rob. "And *they*

need to know that *you* know what's going on and that you care."

It's not unusual for PMI to spend 15 to 18 months in discussion before a partnership deal is struck. "We want to get to know their management; we want to study their systems," explains Rob. "We're looking for great production facilities. We prefer to work with factories where the owner is an engineer rather than a marketer. That's usually a better fit for us because we're the marketing specialists."

After forming a joint venture or partnership with a production facility in Asia, PMI works hard to maintain the relationship. "We don't tend to jump around a lot. When we find a factory we like, we want to stick with it," says Rob. "Our goal is long-term relationships. We like to be minority partners, with a seat on the board. But we don't want to be majority owners. We look for a balanced relationship that will benefit both sides."

It sounds to me like Rob has been putting his old psychotherapy skills to good use, in a larger arena. His initial investment of $1,200 in 1983 has paid off handsomely. In 1992, the company was generating $12 million in annual revenues. The company now generates $62 million in annual revenues and has 116 employees. "We're still small," says Rob. "The way I look at it, we're just getting started."

BALLS!

From my perspective, Rob's accomplishments are the result of his ingrained spunky attitude. Anyone who chucks a steady job in New Jersey to travel around China looking for factories with a certain something deserves our praise.

Speaking of travelers with spunk, the next story is about someone with a highly innovative approach to airport management. She's got her sights set on convincing a traditionally conservative industry to become significantly more spunky.

Adventures of a Modern Marketer

Kiran Jain caught the travel bug when she was a little girl. Her dad owned a sugar cane plantation in Kenya and her family was always on the go, visiting friends and relatives all over Africa and Europe. She's the only person I know who attended boarding schools in the United Kingdom and the Himalayas!

After graduating from Fordham University with a master's degree in business psychology, she went to work for the Jet Vacations division of Air France and stayed with the company for eight years. "I love traveling, so aviation is the perfect business for me," says Kiran.

In her current role as general manager of marketing for Stewart International Airport in Newburgh, New York, she still does plenty of traveling. Her mission is convincing the world's major air carriers that Stewart is a practical alternative to JFK, La Guardia, and Newark airports.

It's not an easy sell. Stewart is just north of the U.S. Military Academy at West Point, in a majestically scenic area known as the Mid-Hudson Valley. The airport is near the intersection of several major highways, but it's still a 90-minute drive from midtown Manhattan. "I tell the air carriers that we're the congestion-free alternative to the New York City airports," says Kiran. "But the New York City airports are established brands. My challenge is overcoming their brand power and positioning Stewart as the smart choice."

Growing up in Kenya and spending most of her life on the road, Kiran doesn't shrink from a challenge. She equates challenge with adventure. "For me, the adventure is going to somewhere far away, meeting with people I don't know, and bringing business back to Stewart."

Like any successful adventurer—or successful marketer, for that matter—Kiran doesn't rush blindly into the unknown. Her marketing strategy has two distinct components because her audience is made up of two distinct segments.

BALLS!

The first segment of her audience comprises executives, managers, decision makers, and key influencers working at the world's numerous air carriers.

 The second segment of her audience comprises the community around Stewart International Airport. That community includes hundreds of organizations in the private and public sectors. It also includes about 2.5 million people living and working within a 60-mile radius of Stewart.

Both components of the marketing strategy are educational in tone, and both emphasize the overall benefits of a large airport that isn't located near a densely populated metropolis. But that's where the similarity ends. The marketing message for the air carriers is that Stewart outperforms the competition in every critical area of airport service, ranging from baggage handling to gate usage.

Kiran's pitch to the air carriers drills down deeply into the economic bedrock of the aviation business, conveying clearly that Stewart understands the unique needs of the flying community and is ready to meet those needs more cost-effectively than any other airport.

"I do a cost-benefit analysis so I can accurately demonstrate how a carrier will make money by flying in and out of Stewart," says Kiran. "The aviation business is all about numbers, and when I tell prospects that Stewart's fees are 80 percent lower than the other airports in our region, I get their attention very quickly."

Being the low-cost provider isn't enough to close deals, however. Usually, there are three more hurdles to clear before a carrier will consider operating at a new airport. "One, there must be a genuine market for the carrier's services. Two, the market must be wealthy enough to support the carrier's fare structure. Three, there must be community support for maintaining a long-term relationship with the carrier."

Building a Community of Support

The need for community support to foster long-term relationships with air carriers drives the second component of the airport's marketing strategy. "In reality, an airport is already a community of service providers working toward a common goal. So the idea of an 'airport community' is quite natural. We've extended the idea to encompass all the possible organizations that could possibly benefit from the airport's success," says Kiran.

Kiran and other airport officials routinely meet with town councils, speak at public forums, work with local development agencies, partner with community groups,

BALLS!

and support civic projects across the region. Kiran's message to the community is that Stewart is more than an airport; it's an engine for economic growth and positive change throughout the Mid-Hudson Valley. "In today's fast-paced world, how can you expect a region to survive economically without a first-class airport?" she asks. "Stewart is our gateway to the world."

Stewart holds the distinction of being the first commercial airport in the United States to be privatized. In 2000, New York State signed a 99-year agreement with National Express, a large transportation firm based in the United Kingdom, which now runs the airport. "The rest of the aviation community is watching us to see if we succeed," she says. "The proof will be in the pudding."

At this point, the pudding tastes pretty good. In 2000, there were only four air carriers operating from Stewart. In 2004, there were seven. By 2006, she predicts, there will be 10, or possibly more.

"Attracting carriers to your airport is a difficult process," she explains. "But getting carriers to increase their daily flights at your airport is even more difficult, because the only way they can increase the number of flights at your airport is by pulling their aircraft out of other airports, or by purchasing new airplanes."

Here again, the numbers show that Stewart is on the right course. In 2000, the airport handled about 45 flights per day. (After the attacks on the World Trade Center on 9/11, flights dropped sharply to 29 per day.) By 2004, however, the number had climbed to 62 flights per day. By 2006, she estimates, there will be 82 flights per day.

The ascent is slow, but steady. National Express doesn't expect miracles from the airport. But Kiran feels the pressure to succeed anyway. Knowing that the company relies on her to deliver results forces her to think and act creatively. As a helicopter touches down noisily on the tarmac outside her office window, she reflects on the career she's chosen.

"You either love this business or you leave it," Kiran says with a smile. "Aviation is far too difficult an occupation for anyone who isn't absolutely passionate about it. If aviation isn't in your blood, forget about it."

I especially like Kiran's story because it seems to me that pursuing a career in aviation requires a special sort of uncritical love for a very turbulent industry. You need to be brave enough to embrace change, authentic enough to follow strict policies, loud enough to be heard over the roar of all those jet engines, and spunky enough to soar higher than your competitors!

BALLS!

Snag the Ideas!

Spunky is about doing the unexpected, going beyond the normal to achieve something truly great. Spunky is Rob Harris trading his job as a psychotherapist for a chance to roam the boondocks of China. Spunky is Jim Koch putting away his Harvard law degree to return to the family business of brewing beer. Spunky is Dan Horton lending Lonnie Benson $350 to start up a pirate phone company in Seattle. Need to get inspired to do something spunky? Try one of these ideas:

❶ *Be spunky and ballsy when you target a specific opportunity.*

An advertising agency, DNA Brand Mechanics, helped a client target the customers of a rival software firm. They created "fraternity paddles" branded with the client's logo and wrapped each paddle in an oversize brown paper envelope with the words "Assume the Position" printed on the outside. Then the agency mailed the paddles to the competitor's customers, right before a major software upgrade. The message printed on the paddle asked, "Why submit to another painful and expensive upgrade?" and urged switching to their client, which offered a Web-based solution. "And never, ever get slapped with another upgrade," the message promised. It was a

spunky campaign that quickly generated appointments and sales for DNA's client.

❷ *Create a weekly gimmick—and track the results in real time.*
Successful auto dealerships reserve some of their toll-free numbers to use for a special "gimmick of the week." They display the toll-free numbers on their web sites, in print ads, or on TV and radio spots. Since the toll-free numbers can be automatically tracked, the dealers can tell immediately whether the gimmick works. They can also tell who's calling, and from where. Anyone with a retail business can use this technique. It really works, too!

❸ *Don't mail gifts.*
Hand them to your clients or prospects in a face-to-face meeting. Diane Tice of the Pacific Institute once personally flew a package to Australia and hand delivered it to one of their partners simply because they had forgotten to send it a few days earlier and she personally wanted to make amends. If you absolutely have to put something in the mail, make sure it will grab everyone's attention. One of our clients, an innovative marketer at a financial services firm, sent freshly baked apple pies to clients with high potential value. She followed up by sending each client a knife and a fork. Then she sent a note that said, "We don't want a slice of your business. We want the whole pie." The campaign was extremely effective. Who can resist the power of an apple pie?

148

④ *Combine opposites.*

Mix genres. Ignore the common wisdom. New York–based Fearless Entertainment is a leader in a new industry called branded entertainment. Fearless blends pop music with event marketing and new media to produce one-of-a-kind programming such as AT&T Wireless presents Hard Rock Live on MTV, The Experience Concert Series presented by Sony Ericsson on VH1, and The Hard Rock Vault Mobile Truck Tour sponsored by Nokia. Fearless recently created a new music format with select Atlantic Records artists offered for sale on multimedia cards through AT&T Wireless stores. The two industries are blended equally rather than there being a traditional sponsorship arrangement. Target Corporation is another great example of combining opposites. Target decided to turn the fact that the stores carry so many different and often unrelated product lines into an advantage by actively showing and promoting wildly different products in television spots.

Rule 6 — ! is for Go!

You read this book for a reason: to snag a few good ideas and make them your own. So, what are you waiting for? *Get Going!*

("The **biggest** sin is sitting on your ass."

~ Florynce Kennedy)

Seriously, put down the book. This rule is simply *go* start doing something ballsy.

Make a list of three wildly innovative and incredibly profitable projects that you're going to start working on *today*. Write down when you'll actually complete them. Number the projects ❶❷❸ Or name them after your kids. Or your dogs.

Now go begin working on Project Fido. *Go!*

Try it, you'll like it. You'll make your company
money.

BALLS!

You'll make money.

Okay, maybe you won't make money, but you'll learn something from it that may end up making you boatloads of cash down the road.

You're still reading. Stop. Now. Please?

All right. So you're still looking for more inspiration. By virtue of completing this book, I declare you to be a full-fledged person with *Balls!* Visit www.ballssixrules.com to read more stories from businesses across the country and all over the world that have followed the rules—and broken a few—on their way to success. This chapter doesn't give you ideas to snag but instead encourages you to submit your own unique idea for others to use. Tell us how you took one of ours and made it your own. If you do, we'll even send you some of our bouncy blue balls. Maybe you'll even earn a theme song.

If you don't feel like going online, call us toll-free at 1-877-6 Rules Book (1-877-678-5372) to find out more about Lonnie, John, Dan, Wally, Manny, or any company mentioned in the book. We'd like to get to know you, and we'd love an excuse to send you a fishbowl filled with balls. Or a mannequin. Or a Hawaiian shirt. . . .

(Ballsy Reading)

Blanchard, Ken, and Mark Miller. *The Secret: What Great Leaders Know—and Do.* Berrett-Koehler Publishers.

Blanchard, Ken, and Sheldon Bowles. *High Five! The Magic of Working Together.* New York: William Morrow.

Buckingham, Marcus, and Curt Coffman. *First, Break All the Rules: What the World's Greatest Managers Do Differently.* Simon & Schuster.

Collins, Jim. *Good to Great: Why Some Companies Make the Leap . . . and Others Don't.* New York: HarperBusiness.

Fox, Jeffrey J. *How to Become a Great Boss: The Rules for Getting and Keeping the Best Employees.* New York: Hyperion.

Fox, Jeffrey J. *How to Become a Marketing Superstar: Unexpected Rules That Ring the Cash Register.* New York: Hyperion.

Fox, Jeffrey J. *How to Become a Rainmaker: The Rules for Getting and Keeping Customers and Clients.* New York: Hyperion.

Godin, Seth. *Purple Cow: Transform Your Business by Being Remarkable.* Portfolio.

Godin, Seth. *Unleashing the Ideavirus.* New York: Hyperion.

Goleman, Daniel, Richard Boyatzis, and Annie McKee. *Primal Leadership: Realizing the Power of Emotional Intelligence.* Boston: Harvard Business School Press.

Hagel, John, III and Arthur G. Armstrong. *Net Gain: Expanding Markets through Virtual Communities.* Boston: Harvard Business School Press.

Maxwell, John C. *The 21 Indispensable Qualities of a Leader: Becoming the Person Others Will Want to Follow.* Nelson Books.

Maxwell, John C. *The 21 Irrefutable Laws of Leadership.* Nelson Books.

Moore, Geoffrey A. *Crossing the Chasm.* New York: HarperBusiness.

Ries, Al, and Laura Ries. *The 22 Immutable Laws of Branding.* New York: HarperBusiness.

Ries, Al, and Jack Trout. *The 22 Immutable Laws of Marketing: Violate Them at Your Own Risk.* New York: HarperCollins.

Sanders, Tim. *The Likeability Factor: How to Boost Your L-Factor and Achieve Your Life's Dreams.* New York: Crown, 2005.

Sanders, Tim. *Love Is the Killer App: How to Win Business and Influence Friends.* Three Rivers Press.

Tice, Lou. *Smart Talk for Achieving Your Potential: 5 Steps to Get You from Here to There.* Pacific Institute Publishing.

Trout, Jack. *Differentiate or Die: Survival in Our Era of Killer Competition.* John Wiley & Sons.

Ventrice, Cindy. *Make Their Day! Employee Recognition That Works.* Berrett-Koehler Publishers.

Ballsy Reading

(Notes)

Most of the content in this book is based on my own experiences at Who's Calling and other firms where I have worked. The individual stories are based on interviews we conducted with top executives or key players at various companies across the United States. All the stories were vetted for accuracy by the people we interviewed and quoted, or by their representatives. Many, but not all, of the companies featured in this book are clients of Who's Calling. Despite our relationships with these companies, we have been as honest and candid as possible in our portrayal of the challenges they encountered and the strategies they developed to overcome those challenges.

Rule *0* — B is for Brave

Our story of Lonnie Benson and his various business ventures was based primarily on extensive interviews with Lonnie, Wally Rex, and Dan Horton conducted in January and February 2004.

Our story about Marquis Jet Partners was based primarily on an interview with Ken Austin conducted in May 2004. The story also includes information culled from the company's web site, as well as from articles about the company that appeared in *Crain's New York Business*, the *Robb Report*, and *The Source*.

Our story about Jim Koch and the creation of The Boston Beer Company was based on an interview with Jim conducted in September 2004. It also includes information from the company web site and company press materials.

Rule *2* — A is for Authentic

Our story about John F. Stapleton was based on in-depth interviews with John conducted in January and June 2004, and on my own knowledge of John's pivotal role at Who's Calling.

Our story about Perimeter Internetworking was based primarily on an extensive interview conducted with Brad Miller in June 2004. It also includes information from the company web site.

Our story about Da Vinci Gourmet was based on an in-depth interview with Leanna Mix in July 2004. Darcey Howard and Tracy Ging also contributed valuable insight to the story, which includes information and background from the company web site.

Rule ③—L is for Loud

Our stories about the over-the-top marketing efforts of the marketing team at Who's Calling are based on numerous extensive and exhaustive interviews with members of the Who's Calling staff conducted from January to September 2004, my actual experience over the past four years, plus a ton of e-mail messages to and from anyone who ever participated in one of our unforgettable events! Our story about salesforce.com's in-your-face marketing tactics was based primarily on an interview with Parker Harris conducted in August 2004.

Our story about Pacific Market International's innovative *PMI Trend Perspective* was based on interviews conducted with Tami Fujii in August 2004.

Rule ④—L is for Lovable

Our stories about Who's Calling and its unique approaches to human resources and customer relationship management are based on a series of extensive interviews with members of the Who's Calling staff conducted from January to September 2004.

Our brief anecdote about Marc Benioff and the altruistic side of salesforce.com was culled from information on the company web site.

Our story about Jack Shimota and the customer-friendly culture at Walser Automotive Group was based primarily on an interview with Jack conducted in May 2004. It is also based on our staff's collective knowledge of Walser, which has been a Who's Calling client for many years.

Our story about *duPont Registry* magazine was based primarily on an in-depth interview conducted with Kit Jeerapaet in June 2004.

Rule *6*—S is for Spunky

Our story about Kate Stapleton and the MARs process was based primarily on a series of in-depth interviews conducted with Kate, Ed Parkinson, and Matt Stroh in August and September 2004.

Our stories about the Bleed Blue Tours and our Catalyst certification program were based on extensive interviews conducted with JoAnn Bercot, Kate Stapleton, Wally Rex, Dave Venneri, and Matt Stroh in September 2004.

Our story about the sales force reorganization was based on in-depth interviews conducted with John Stapleton and Dave Venneri from January to September 2004. Our story about the creation of Pacific Market International was based primarily on several interviews with Rob Harris conducted in August and September 2004. Tami

Fujii also contributed vital information to this excellent and intriguing story.

Our story about Stewart International Airport was based primarily on an in-depth interview conducted with Kiran Jain in September 2004.

A few days before *Balls!* went to press, we learned that Kiran had accepted a position as director of marketing at Bradley International Airport, near Hartford, Connecticut. Bradley, which serves more than 6.25 million passengers annually, is a much larger operation than Stewart. Kiran's new job is definitely a big step up. She'll also face a bunch of new challenges, since Bradley is a public entity and Stewart was privately owned. But I'm certain that Kiran will succeed—after all, she has *Balls!*

Acknowledgments

Balls! was written with the help and support of many great friends, wonderful colleagues, and truly extraordinary clients who shared their time, energy, and amazing stories. Thanks are due to all the employees and members of the executive management team at Who's Calling. Without their genuine interest and encouragement, this project could not have taken flight. Special thanks to Lonnie Benson, John Stapleton, Dan Horton, Wally Rex, and Amy Ziegenbein for sharing their experiences in such wonderful detail.

Balls! is really a collection of fascinating stories from the front lines of business. I want to thank all the people who contributed insight and anecdotes, including Jack Shimota, Kit Jeerapaet, Tami Fujii, Rob Harris, Ken Austin, Bill Allard, Kenny Dichter, Jesse Itzler, Brad Miller, Andy Greenawalt, Darcey Howard, Leanna Mix, Marc Benioff, Parker Harris, Jim Koch, Kiran Jain, Bill Donges, Jared Miller, Matt Reynolds, Ted Loughead, Cathy Ellico, Bill Krouse, Jeff Schrier, Alan Brown, Dan Gross, Chase Fraser, Lou and Diane Tice, Stuart DePina, Bill Carleton,

Richard Counihan, Tara Butler, Ed Parkinson, Tracey Riper, Matt Stroh, Kate Stapleton, Shellie Pierce, Holly Crace, Diane Hager, Shyan Griffith, Bryan Reidy, JoAnn Bercot, Mark Mansfield, Karen Jansen, Teresa Bordenet, Sean Stapleton, Kelly Curran, Robert Fundy, and Ali Reynolds.

I owe a special debt of gratitude to Mike Barlow, our editorial director, who kept the project on course and didn't shy away from all the ballsy ideas. Mike is an excellent writer, a great editor, and a motivational coach who kept us all focused and on task.

Kudos also to our incredible design team of Jeanette Cooper, Herb Collingridge, and Tricia Diaz for creating ballsy designs that brought extra life to the words.

I also want to thank Matt Holt, our editor at John Wiley & Sons, and his wonderful assistant, Tamara Hummel. Matt and Tamara did a great job of supporting and encouraging my creative vision, and for that I am deeply grateful!

Most of all, I want to thank my husband, Dave Venneri, for putting up with the long hours of brainstorming, writing, and editing. Without his incredible support and the late-night company of our two beagles, Kayla and Matilda, we wouldn't have *Balls!*

(Index)

171

173

175